Master Management & Leadership Skills

Develop Emotional Intelligence for Enhanced Communication, improve Workload Balance and Reduce Stress to lead your team with confidence.

Wendy Williams

Red Squirrel Publishing

Table of Contents

Enjoyed This Book? Join Us in The Literary Lounge!

Dear Reader,
Thank you for purchasing this book. We hope it inspired you, taught you, and gave you plenty of moments to reflect on.
If you're looking for more great reads, insights, and a community of curious minds, we'd love to invite you to join The Literary Lounge, our FREE exclusive book club for non-fiction lovers.
As a member, you'll receive:
First access to new releases – be the first to dive into our latest non-fiction titles!
Exclusive freebies and content – enjoy monthly downloads, behind-the-scenes stories, and more.
Special book promotions – get insider tips on upcoming promotions and grab your next read for free.
Join us today and stay connected to a world of thought-provoking books, great conversations, and a community of fellow readers.

__click the link to join The Literary Lounge!

Or scan the QR code

We can't wait to welcome you!

Happy Reading,

The Literary Lounge Team

Introduction

In my years of management, I've faced challenges that tested every skill I thought I had. One particular moment stands out—a time when my once-thriving team had become fragmented and unmotivated. Miscommunication was rife, deadlines slipped, and a sense of unease began to take hold. Despite my experience, I found myself questioning my ability to lead in this shifting environment. It was a turning point that forced me to rethink my approach, adapt, and grow as a leader. This experience mirrors the challenges many managers face today.

The modern workplace is fraught with complexities. Managers grapple with poor communication, decision-making paralysis, lack of team cohesion, and ethical dilemmas. These challenges are not merely obstacles; they are barriers that can hinder personal and organizational growth. Effective management skills are no longer a luxury but a necessity. They are the bedrock upon which successful teams and thriving organizations are built.

This book is a comprehensive toolkit for managers at every stage of their careers. Whether you're looking to refine established skills or seeking guidance as a new leader, the insights and strategies shared here are designed to help you confidently navigate the complexities of management. From improving communication and decision-making to managing stress and fostering personal growth, this resource is packed with practical advice to support your leadership journey.

This book's target audience is broad yet specific. It caters to existing managers eager to elevate their skills, new managers who need a roadmap, and students studying management. Each group faces unique challenges, but they share a common goal: to lead effectively and achieve excellence in their roles.

This book's content is meticulously structured to provide a holistic approach to management. Each chapter focuses on a critical aspect of effective management. We begin with the cornerstone of all successful leadership: effective communication. You will learn techniques to enhance your verbal and nonverbal communication, engage in active listening, and foster an environment of open dialogue.

Next, we delve into emotional intelligence, exploring how self-awareness, empathy, and social skills can transform one's leadership style. This chapter will provide insights into understanding one's emotions and those of one's team, leading to more harmonious and productive interactions.

Ethical leadership is another vital component addressed in this book. In an era where ethical lapses can have far-reaching consequences, understanding the principles of ethical decision-making is paramount. You will learn how to navigate complex ethical dilemmas, build a culture of integrity, and lead by example.

Team building is covered extensively, offering strategies to foster collaboration, enhance team dynamics, and create a sense of belonging among team members. You'll discover the importance of trust, respect, and shared goals in building a high-performing team.

We also tackle the often-overlooked aspect of stress management. High-pressure environments are common today, and managing stress effectively is crucial for personal well-being and team performance. This chapter provides practical techniques for managing stress, maintaining work-life balance, and creating a supportive work environment.

Continuous learning is the final piece of the puzzle. In a rapidly changing world, the ability to learn and adapt is critical for any manager. This chapter emphasizes the importance of lifelong learning, offering strategies to stay updated with industry trends, develop new skills, and foster a culture of continuous improvement within your team.

Allow me to introduce myself. I am the author, driven by a passion for helping adults, managers, supervisors, and students overcome the challenges of leading teams and achieving excellence. My management journey began when I was just 18, straight out of college, when I took on the role of Trainee Manager at Berni Inns in 1980 (yes, I'm that old!). Since then, I've gained a wealth of experience across various roles and industries.

I've managed teams in different capacities throughout the years, learning the ropes of leadership, communication, and decision-making. From those early days as a trainee manager to running my businesses and employing staff, I've faced countless challenges, made my share of mistakes, and grown as a leader. These experiences have given me valuable insights into what it takes to be an effective manager, and I'm excited to share that knowledge with you.

In semi-retirement, I've turned my attention to publishing books to pass on what I've learned. My goal is to help others like you navigate the complex world of management with the benefit of the lessons I've accumulated over the years. With the right tools and guidance, anyone can become a successful manager, and I'm here to support you on that journey.

This book promises practicality. It offers actionable steps, practical exercises, and real-life case studies, ensuring that the content is informative and easy to follow and implement in real-world scenarios. Additionally, you will have access to 14 free downloadable resources, providing further support and making it a valuable reference. These tools and guidance make this book an efficient and relevant resource that can be applied directly to your daily management practices.

As you read this book, you can expect to acquire essential management skills, apply them effectively, and be equipped to handle various management challenges confidently. The insights and strategies shared in these pages are designed to empower you, enabling you to lead confidently and achieve remarkable results.

I encourage you to commit to your personal and professional development. Actively engage with the content, complete the exercises, and apply the insights to your daily management practices. Your journey to becoming an exceptional manager begins here, and the possibilities for growth and success are limitless. The path to effective leadership is not always easy, but with dedication and the right tools, you can overcome any challenge and lead your team to new heights.

Foundations of Effective Management

When I stepped into my first role as a young catering manager, I was eager but quickly overwhelmed by the responsibilities of managing a sizable team of different ages and skill sets. While I was full of enthusiasm, I soon realized that being a manager was about far more than simply delegating tasks or overseeing daily operations. It required understanding the nuances of leadership, mentorship, and strategic thinking to bring out the best in the team.

This experience highlighted the multifaceted nature of effective management—a theme that we'll explore in detail throughout this chapter.

You have many roles

Understanding Your Role as a Manager

As a manager, your role transcends the simplistic notion of being a taskmaster. You are a leader, a mentor, and a strategist, each facet interwoven to create a cohesive approach to management. Though often used interchangeably, leadership and management differ significantly. Leadership involves inspiring and guiding your team towards a shared vision, fostering a sense of purpose and motivation. On the other hand, management is about orchestrating day-to-day operations to achieve specific goals, ensuring that tasks are completed efficiently and effectively. Balancing these roles requires you to navigate short-term tasks while keeping an eye on long-term objectives, a delicate equilibrium that defines successful management.

Managers' responsibilities are diverse and demanding. Planning and setting objectives are at the heart of what we do, requiring clear, measurable goals that align with the organization's wider vision. In my early management experiences, I learned that creating these goals wasn't just about ticking boxes—it was about ensuring they inspired the team and gave them a clear sense of purpose.

Equally important is organizing and delegating tasks. This means carefully allocating resources, matching tasks to each team member's strengths, and ensuring that everyone understands their roles and responsibilities. I quickly discovered that when people feel empowered by the tasks they're given, their performance thrives.

Monitoring and assessing performance is another key responsibility. Whether through regular check-ins, feedback sessions, or formal reviews, staying connected with your team ensures progress stays on track and any issues are addressed early. These fundamentals, while challenging at first, are the building blocks for managing effectively.

Adaptability is a hallmark of effective management. In today's rapidly evolving business landscape, whether you're leading a small to medium-sized enterprise (SME) or a large corporation, the ability to pivot and adjust your approach is essential; flexibility is not just advantageous but necessary. Navigating organizational changes, whether from internal restructuring or external market shifts, demands a proactive and resilient approach. Adapting to different team dynamics is equally crucial; understanding each team member's unique strengths, weaknesses, and motivations allows you to tailor your management style to maximize productivity and morale.

The impact of effective management extends beyond the confines of your immediate team. A well-managed team operates like a finely tuned machine, where each member understands their role and works collaboratively towards common goals. This synergy enhances overall performance, boosts morale, and fosters a positive work environment. Moreover, effective management contributes to the organization's success by ensuring that projects are completed on time, resources are used efficiently, and strategic objectives are met. In essence, your role as a manager is pivotal, influencing not only the success of your team but also the broader organizational outcomes.

Understanding Your Management Style

Understanding one's management style is paramount for effective leadership (Evans, 2022).[1] A manager's style profoundly influences their team's morale, productivity, and overall success. Recognizing whether you are more autocratic, democratic, or laissez-faire in your approach allows you to harness your strengths and address your weaknesses, thereby enhancing your leadership effectiveness. Each style has its merits and demerits; for instance, an autocratic manager excels in decision-making speed but may stifle creativity, whereas a democratic manager fosters collaboration yet might experience slower decision-making processes. By comprehending your natural inclinations, you can tailor your approach to fit the unique needs of your team and the specific demands of various situations.

Self-awareness in a manager's approach is essential for creating a positive workplace. By understanding their management style, managers can anticipate how their team will react to their decisions. This insight is particularly beneficial in identifying environments where a collaborative approach, valuing teamwork and collective input, nurtures a culture of inclusion and mutual respect. Alternatively, scenarios that demand swift, decisive action may require a more directive management style. Recognizing and adapting to these varying needs enhances team dynamics and empowers managers to lead effectively across various situations, from navigating crises to managing daily operations.

One of my first managers leaned heavily on a laissez-faire approach. I initially loved his style—he was approachable and easy-going and gave us plenty of freedom to explore ideas and innovate. At first, it felt like an ideal environment. However, as time passed, I noticed that some less experienced team members were struggling. Without enough direction or support, they often felt lost and unsure of their next steps, which led to confusion.

This experience taught me a valuable lesson about leadership. While the hands-off approach worked well for those with more experience, it didn't suit everyone. Over time, my manager recognized this and started adapting his style, providing more structure and guidance when needed. The change made a huge difference, especially for those team members who needed more support. Looking back, I saw how his flexibility was the hallmark of effective leadership—the ability to adapt to the needs of the team and the situation at hand.

Self-Evaluation Tools for Managers

Self-evaluation is the cornerstone of continuous improvement and heightened self-awareness, allowing managers to introspect and calibrate their strategies (Garcia, 2021).[2] Self-assessment is not merely an academic exercise but a practical necessity for those who aim to refine their leadership capabilities. It provides a structured method to scrutinize one's strengths and identify areas needing enhancement, fostering a culture of self-improvement. This process demands honesty and objectivity, encouraging managers to confront their limitations and celebrate their competencies, laying the groundwork for personal and professional development.

Various self-evaluation tools can aid in this introspective journey. *The SWOT analysis, for instance, offers a comprehensive overview by categorizing. This tool enables managers to devise strategies that leverage their strengths while addressing weaknesses. Complementing this, the 360-degree feedback mechanism collects insights from peers, subordinates, and supervisors, offering a holistic perspective on performance and interpersonal skills (a).* Emotional intelligence tests, such as the Emotional Intelligence EQ, further illuminate self-awareness, self-regulation, empathy, and social skills, which are crucial for effective leadership. These tools collectively provide a multi-faceted understanding of one's management style and effectiveness.

Interpreting the results of these evaluations necessitates a systematic approach. Managers must sift through the feedback to discern patterns and recurring themes, often highlighting core development areas. Strengths identified should be harnessed to drive team performance, while weaknesses should be targeted with specific improvement plans. For instance, if a manager discovers through a 360-degree feedback survey that their communication skills need enhancement, they might invest in targeted communication training or seek mentorship. These insights are not ends in themselves but serve as catalysts for creating robust, actionable personal improvement plans, ensuring that the manager evolves in their role, adapting to new challenges with agility and insight.

Setting Clear Expectations and Goals

The significance of clear communication in setting expectations cannot be overstated. It is the foundation upon which team performance and morale are built. When expectations are explicitly defined, misunderstandings are minimized, and team members are less likely to misinterpret instructions or objectives. This clarity fosters an environment where accountability thrives, as each individual understands their responsibilities and the benchmarks against which their performance will be measured.

Implementing the SMART framework—Specific, Measurable, Achievable, Relevant, Time-bound—is an effective technique for setting goals (Martinez, 2020) (b).[3] Specific goals delineate precise outcomes, leaving no room for ambiguity. Measurable goals establish clear criteria for success, allowing progress to be tracked with tangible metrics. Achievable goals ensure realistic objectives, considering the team's capabilities and resources. Relevant goals align with broader business objectives, providing context and significance. Time-bound goals with defined deadlines create a sense of urgency and focus, ensuring that milestones are met within the designated timeframe.

Aligning individual and team goals with organizational objectives is a critical process that ensures coherence and unity in efforts. This alignment involves cascading goals from the managerial level to individual contributors, ensuring that each team member's objectives support the broader mission. Regular reviews are imperative to maintain this alignment, allowing for adjustments as organizational priorities evolve. These reviews foster a dynamic goal-setting environment where objectives remain relevant and achievable.

Continuous communication and feedback are vital in the goal-setting process. Weekly progress meetings provide a forum for discussing achievements, addressing challenges, and recalibrating efforts. Real-time feedback mechanisms, such as instant messaging or collaborative platforms, facilitate immediate communication, ensuring that issues are promptly addressed and successes swiftly acknowledged.

Building Trust and Credibility

Acting with integrity is not merely a moral obligation but a strategic imperative. Managers who consistently demonstrate honesty, fairness, and ethical conduct engender trust within their teams, creating a foundation of mutual respect and reliability. Transparency in decision-making further fortifies this trust. When managers are open about their thought processes, rationale, and the factors influencing their decisions, it demystifies leadership actions and fosters an environment where team members feel valued and informed.

Additionally, transparency in decision-making strengthens this trust. When managers are open about their thought processes, reasoning, and the factors influencing their decisions, they clarify their actions and foster an environment where team members feel valued and informed.

Consistency and reliability are equally paramount in building credibility. A manager's word must be their bond; following through on commitments, regardless of scale, establishes a reputation for dependability. This reliability must permeate minor and significant tasks, affirming that the manager is steadfast and trustworthy in all professional undertakings. For instance, a manager who consistently meets deadlines and delivers on promises, whether a small task like providing feedback or a substantial project milestone, will naturally cultivate an aura of credibility and trustworthiness.

Open and honest communication serves as the lifeblood of trust within a team. Encouraging open dialogue allows for the free exchange of ideas, concerns, and feedback, which enhances transparency and builds a collaborative culture. Addressing issues transparently, without obfuscation or delay, signals to team members that their concerns are taken seriously and that the manager values their input. This approach mitigates misunderstandings and preempts conflicts, fostering an atmosphere of openness and mutual respect.

Building relationships through empathy and understanding is the capstone of trust-building. Active listening, where managers genuinely engage with and consider their team members' perspectives, demonstrates respect and appreciation. This involves not just hearing words but comprehending the underlying emotions and motivations. Showing genuine concern for team members' well-being through personal check-ins or supportive actions during challenging times cements the relational bonds. It reinforces the manager's perception as a compassionate and empathetic leader.

Time Management Techniques for Managers

Effective time management is a cornerstone of successful leadership. While detailed strategies are covered in Chapter 12, it's essential to highlight a few foundational techniques here.

Prioritization is critical for managers. Tools like the Eisenhower Matrix and ABCDE Method help categorize tasks, allowing you to focus on what truly matters. For instance, by distinguishing tasks based on urgency and importance, managers can align their efforts with strategic objectives and reduce wasted time. Delegation also plays a vital role, enabling managers to empower their teams and focus on higher-level responsibilities. Assigning tasks that foster team growth can create a more balanced and efficient workload.

Productivity techniques such as time-blocking and digital tools can help streamline workflows. Managers can enhance collaboration and maintain clarity by setting aside dedicated time for specific tasks and using tools like Trello or Asana. Finding a work-life balance is crucial for sustaining long-term productivity and avoiding burnout. Chapter 12 delves deeper into methods and exercises for achieving an optimal balance between work and personal life.

Chapter 12 comprehensively explores these strategies, including the Eisenhower Matrix, ABCDE Method, delegation best practices, and work-life balance tips.

Downloadable Resources

To complement this chapter, the following resources are available for download at the end of Chapter 15:

a. SWOT Analysis – A practical guide to identify strengths, weaknesses, opportunities, and threats.

b. SMART Framework – A guide to assess and improve goal setting.

Mastering Communication Skills

Imagine a scenario where Maria, a department head at a thriving tech startup, finds herself in a critical meeting with her team to discuss an impending product launch. Despite her expertise and enthusiasm, the meeting quickly derails as team members talk over each other, misunderstandings abound, and crucial points are lost in the chaos. Maria realizes that her well-intentioned directives are not resonating, leading to frustration and inefficiency. This situation underscores the pivotal role that adept communication plays in effective management. Communication is about delivering messages and ensuring they are received, understood, and acted upon appropriately.

Active Listening for Better Understanding

Active listening is the bedrock of effective communication. This involves more than just nodding; it requires an intentional focus on the speaker's words and non-verbal cues, ensuring a comprehensive understanding of their message. Active listening entails absorbing the information presented and engaging with it, reflecting on it, and responding thoughtfully. When you focus entirely on the speaker, you create an environment where they feel heard and valued, fostering a sense of mutual respect and trust. Avoiding premature judgments is equally crucial, as it allows you to remain open to the speaker's perspective, free from preconceived notions or biases that could cloud your understanding.

Techniques for active listening can significantly enhance your ability to connect with others (Garcia, 2021).[1] Paraphrasing and summarizing are invaluable tools in this regard. By rephrasing the speaker's message in your own words and summarizing key points, you confirm your understanding and demonstrate that you are actively engaged in the conversation. Non-verbal cues, such as nodding and maintaining eye contact, further reinforce your attentiveness and empathy. These cues signal the speaker that you are fully present, encouraging a more open and honest dialogue. Additionally, asking clarifying questions can help you delve deeper into the speaker's message, uncovering nuances and ensuring you understand their words' full context.

However, active listening is often impeded by various barriers. Multitasking and distractions are common culprits, diverting your attention from the speaker and leading to fragmented understanding. In our digitally connected world, the temptation to check emails or respond to messages during conversations can be particularly strong, but doing so undermines your ability to listen effectively. Preconceived notions and biases also pose significant obstacles, as they can distort your perception of the speaker's message. Overcoming these barriers requires consciously eliminating distractions, approaching each conversation with an open mind, and focusing entirely on the speaker.

The benefits of active listening in management are manifold. By practicing active listening, you can build stronger relationships with your team members, fostering a sense of trust and collaboration. When team members feel that their voices are heard and their input is valued, they are more likely to be engaged and motivated. Active listening also enhances problem-solving by allowing you to fully understand the issues at hand and consider multiple perspectives before arriving at a solution. This comprehensive understanding can lead to more effective and innovative outcomes, as you are better equipped to address the root causes of problems rather than merely treating symptoms.

Which Listener type are you?

Reflection Exercise: Enhancing Active Listening Skills

Consider the last time you felt truly heard in a conversation. Reflect on the other person's behaviors and techniques to make you feel understood and valued. Now, think about a recent conversation where you struggled to listen actively. What barriers did you encounter, and how did they affect the outcome? Use these reflections to identify specific actions to elevate your active listening skills in future interactions.

By honing your active listening abilities, you can transform your communication style, making it more effective and empathetic. This foundational skill will improve your interactions with your team and enhance your overall leadership effectiveness.

Crafting Clear and Concise Messages

Imagine a scenario where you must communicate an urgent strategic shift to your team. A clear and concise message is essential to ensure everyone understands the changes. Using simple, direct language is key to making your message accessible to everyone, regardless of their familiarity with the subject. Avoiding jargon and overly complex terms minimizes the risk of misinterpretation while respecting your team's time and capacity to process information. Clear, straightforward communication fosters understanding, builds trust, and demonstrates consideration for your audience.

The structure of your message is just as important as the words you choose. One effective technique is to present the most critical information upfront, followed by supporting details. This approach lets your audience quickly grasp the main points, even if they don't dive into every detail. Highlighting key elements at the beginning ensures your message isn't lost in the minutiae. This method is especially valuable in fast-paced business environments where time is limited, and focus needs to be sharp. Organizing your communication this way helps ensure that your team remains aligned and informed, even during periods of change or urgency.

Visual aids and supporting materials can significantly enhance the clarity of your message (Evans, 2021).[2] Incorporating charts and graphs for data presentation can make complex information more digestible and visually appealing. These tools help to illustrate trends, patterns, and relationships that might be difficult to convey through text alone. Bullet points are another valuable tool, providing a clear and organized way to present information. They break down complex ideas into manageable chunks, making it easier for your audience to follow and remember the key points. Visual aids support your message and engage your audience, making communication more interactive and effective.

Tailoring your message to suit the audience's needs is critical to effective communication. When addressing non-experts, simplifying the language and avoiding technical jargon is essential. This ensures your message is accessible and understandable, regardless of the audience's background. Conversely, when communicating with experts, using technical terms appropriately can convey respect for their knowledge and facilitate a more in-depth discussion. Adapting your message to your audience involves understanding their level of expertise, their interests, and their needs. This tailored approach not only enhances comprehension but also builds rapport and trust.

In my role, I've often had to find the right balance between supporting experienced team members and guiding those new to the role. I remember introducing a new initiative to the team, and it became clear that explaining things too technically would only overwhelm the less experienced members. So, I adjusted my approach, breaking down the concepts into simple terms and using analogies that made the ideas easier to understand. I wanted them to feel confident and engaged, not lost in jargon.

On the other hand, with my more seasoned team members, I took a different approach. I'd delve into the technical details, using industry-specific language to acknowledge their expertise and open the door for in-depth discussions. This approach respected their experience and invited them to bring their insights forward.

Balancing these communication styles allowed me to ensure that everyone—regardless of experience—understood the initiative and felt included in the process. Over time, this has become one of my key strategies for building a unified and engaged team.

The principles of clear communication involve the words you use and how you organize and present those words. By using simple and direct language, structuring your messages effectively, incorporating visual aids, and tailoring your communication to your audience, you can ensure that your messages are clear, concise, impactful, and memorable.

> "Most people do not listen with the intent to understand; they listen with the intent to reply."
> – Stephen R. Covey

Providing Constructive Feedback

Providing feedback is one of the most valuable tools in a manager's toolkit. It's not about chastising but guiding team members toward improved performance and professional growth. Effective feedback is specific and focuses on behavior rather than personality. For instance, instead of saying, "You need to be more punctual," you could say, "I've noticed that you

were late to three meetings this week, which affected our project timelines."
This approach makes the issue clear and actionable, helping the recipient
understand and address the specific behavior.

Taking a balanced approach to feedback is just as important.
Acknowledging positive behaviors alongside areas for improvement
creates a well-rounded perspective that encourages growth without
discouraging the individual. One effective technique is the "Sandwich
Method," where you begin with positive feedback, introduce the
constructive critique, and end with another positive comment. For
example, you might say, "Your presentation was engaging and
well-researched. However, there were a few instances where the data wasn't
as clear as it could have been. Overall, your ability to captivate the audience
was impressive, and with more clarity in your data, it will be exceptional."
This method softens the impact of the critique, making it more likely to be
received positively while maintaining a focus on growth and improvement.

Delivering feedback effectively requires what you say and how you say it.
Using "I" statements to express observations can mitigate defensiveness
and make the feedback feel less like an attack. For example, "I noticed that
the report was submitted past the deadline, which impacted our project
schedule," is more constructive than, "You missed the deadline again." This
subtle language shift can significantly affect how the feedback is received
and acted upon.

Equally important is the manager's ability to receive feedback gracefully.
Demonstrating openness and a willingness to improve sets a powerful
example for the team. Encouraging team members to share their views
fosters a culture where feedback is a two-way street, enhancing mutual
respect and continuous improvement. Managers should actively solicit
feedback, perhaps through regular check-ins or anonymous surveys, and
respond to it constructively, showing that they value and consider their
team's input.

Creating a feedback culture within the organization involves more than
just occasional feedback sessions. It requires a systematic approach
where feedback is a regular, valued practice. Implementing regular
feedback sessions, such as quarterly reviews or monthly one-on-ones,
ensures that feedback is timely and relevant. Recognizing and rewarding
constructive feedback, both given and received, can further reinforce its
importance. This might involve publicly acknowledging team members

who provide insightful feedback or celebrating those who show significant improvement following feedback.

By embedding these practices into the daily fabric of team interactions, you can cultivate an environment where feedback is not feared but welcomed and where every team member feels equipped to grow and excel. This culture of continuous feedback will enhance individual performance and drive collective success, fostering a more cohesive, high-performing team.

Navigating Difficult Conversations

Preparing for difficult conversations requires a blend of emotional intelligence and strategic foresight. Before engaging in a challenging discussion, setting clear objectives for the conversation is imperative (Harris, 2022).[3] This involves pinpointing the core issues you intend to address and the outcomes you hope to achieve. For instance, if the topic is an employee's declining performance, your objectives might include understanding the underlying reasons, providing constructive feedback, and collaboratively devising an improvement plan. Anticipating potential reactions and responses is equally crucial. Consider the emotional and psychological state of the other party, and prepare for a range of responses—from defensive posturing to emotional outbursts. By visualizing these scenarios, you can formulate responses that keep the dialogue constructive and focused on resolution.

Maintaining composure during challenging interactions is a skill that can be honed through practice and mindfulness techniques. Deep breathing exercises are a simple yet effective way to calm your nerves, ensuring you remain composed and centered. Before responding to any provocative statement or unexpected reaction, take a moment to pause and collect your thoughts. This brief interlude allows you to process the information and respond thoughtfully rather than reacting impulsively. Another helpful technique is to keep your tone measured and your body language open, which helps to de-escalate tension and foster a more collaborative atmosphere.

Resolving conflicts constructively involves a series of strategic steps to find common ground and address underlying issues. Begin by identifying shared goals and mutual interests, which can be a foundation for collaborative problem-solving. For example, in a conflict between two team members, emphasize their common objective of contributing to the team's success. Mediation techniques can be invaluable in this context. You can guide the conversation as a neutral facilitator, ensuring both parties feel heard and understood. This might involve setting ground rules for respectful dialogue, actively listening to each party's perspective, and encouraging them to propose solutions. The goal is to shift the focus from assigning blame to finding a mutually acceptable resolution.

Follow-up actions post-conversation are critical to ensuring the agreed-upon resolutions are implemented and sustained. Documenting agreements and action items record what was discussed and decided, serving as a reference point for future interactions. This documentation should include specific actions, responsible parties, and timelines, ensuring accountability. Scheduling regular check-ins to monitor progress is equally important. These follow-ups allow you to assess whether the agreed-upon actions are being carried out, address emerging issues, and provide ongoing support. By maintaining open lines of communication, you reinforce the commitment to resolving the conflict and fostering a positive work environment.

Navigating difficult conversations with skill and empathy resolves immediate issues, strengthens relationships, and builds a culture of trust and openness. As you master these techniques, you will find that even the most challenging discussions can become opportunities for growth and improvement. In the next chapter, we will delve into the intricacies of emotional intelligence and its profound impact on effective management, exploring how self-awareness, empathy, and social skills can transform your leadership approach.

Emotional Intelligence in Management

A seasoned manager named David faced a critical challenge in a busy warehouse. Tasked with leading a cross-departmental team on a high-priority logistics project, he had to balance the technical demands of optimizing workflows with the human dynamics of his diverse team. Tempers flared as deadlines loomed, and differing department priorities added to the strain. David quickly realized that technical expertise alone wouldn't resolve these challenges. To succeed, he needed to tap into a deeper understanding of emotions—his own and his team's. By acknowledging their frustrations and pressures, he began fostering a sense of trust and collaboration, turning potential conflict into a unified effort.

Self-Awareness: The First Step to Emotional Intelligence

Self-awareness, the cornerstone of emotional intelligence, is the conscious knowledge of one's character, feelings, motives, and desires. It involves profoundly recognizing your emotions and understanding how they influence your behavior and decision-making. This awareness is not merely reflective but extends to an accurate appraisal of your strengths and weaknesses, enabling you to navigate the complexities of leadership with a balanced perspective. Recognizing your emotions as they arise allows you to manage them effectively, preventing impulsive reactions that could derail your objectives. Understanding your strengths empowers you to leverage them strategically while acknowledging your weaknesses provides opportunities for growth and development.

Enhancing self-awareness involves deliberate practices to foster a deeper understanding of your internal landscape. Keeping a daily journal, where you reflect on your emotions, actions, and their impacts, can be an invaluable tool. This practice allows you to identify patterns in your behavior, uncovering triggers that influence your emotional responses. By documenting and reflecting on your experiences, you gain insights into your emotional triggers and how they shape your interactions with others. Regular feedback from peers and subordinates also plays a crucial role in this process. Constructive feedback offers an external perspective on your actions and decisions, highlighting areas that may be blind spots in your self-perception. Seeking this feedback requires humility and a genuine willingness to improve, fostering a culture of continuous learning and self-improvement.

The benefits of self-awareness in management are far-reaching. When you develop a heightened self-awareness, you can make more informed decisions based on a clear understanding of the situation. It allows you to recognize and manage your emotions and biases, ensuring your decisions are rational and well-considered. This clarity in decision-making strengthens your credibility as a leader, fostering trust and respect within your team.

Self-awareness also plays a crucial role in building authentic relationships. By being attuned to your emotions and behaviors, you can communicate more effectively and empathetically, creating an environment of openness and mutual respect. This authenticity resonates with your team, fostering a culture where trust and collaboration thrive.

Various tools and resources are available to assess and enhance your self-awareness. Emotional intelligence assessments, such as the Emotional and Social Competency Inventory (ESCI), provide a structured framework for evaluating your emotional competencies. These assessments offer insights into your emotional strengths and areas for development, guiding your efforts to enhance your emotional intelligence. Personality tests, like the Emotional Intelligence EQ, also contribute to this self-awareness journey. This test provides a detailed understanding of your personality traits and preferences and how they influence your interactions with others. By integrating the insights from these assessments into your daily practices, you can develop a nuanced understanding of your emotional landscape, paving the way for more effective and empathetic leadership.

Reflective Exercise: Enhancing Self-Awareness through Journaling

Take a few moments at the end of each day to reflect on your emotions and actions. Write down specific instances where your emotions influenced your behavior, and consider how you might respond differently in the future. Identify any recurring patterns and reflect on their impact on your leadership effectiveness. Use these reflections to set intentional goals for improving your emotional responses and interactions with your team.

By embracing the journey of self-awareness, you lay the groundwork for emotional intelligence, equipping yourself with the tools to lead with empathy, clarity, and authenticity. The journey of self-awareness is continuous, requiring ongoing reflection, feedback, and a commitment to personal growth.

Manage your emotions under pressure

Managing Your Emotions Under Pressure

In all work environments, the ability to manage your emotions under pressure is not just a desirable trait but an imperative one. Imagine being in a crucial client meeting when unexpected issues threaten to derail the entire project. Your heart races, your palms sweat, and a surge of anxiety cloud your judgment. In such moments, the capacity to regulate your emotions becomes the linchpin of effective leadership. Emotional regulation involves recognizing your emotional triggers, understanding their impact on your behavior, and employing strategies to manage these emotions constructively.

One effective technique for managing emotions under pressure is the practice of mindfulness (Martinez, 2022).[1] Mindfulness involves paying deliberate attention to the present moment, acknowledging your feelings without judgment, and employing techniques such as deep breathing to maintain calm. For instance, taking a few deep breaths can activate the parasympathetic nervous system, which helps reduce stress and anxiety. This simple yet powerful practice can be particularly useful in high-pressure situations, allowing you to pause, collect your thoughts, and respond rather than react impulsively. By cultivating mindfulness, you can create a mental space that enables you to think clearly and make rational decisions even under duress.

Another crucial strategy is cognitive reframing, which involves changing your perspective on a stressful situation to view it more positively or neutrally. When faced with a challenging scenario, instead of succumbing to negative emotions, try to reframe the situation as an opportunity for growth and learning. For example, rather than viewing a project setback as a failure, consider it a chance to identify weaknesses and improve future performance. This shift in mindset can significantly reduce stress and enhance your ability to manage emotions effectively. Cognitive reframing helps you maintain a balanced outlook, preventing negative emotions from overwhelming your decision-making processes.

Effective time management also plays a vital role in managing emotions under pressure. By organizing your tasks, setting realistic goals, and prioritizing your responsibilities, you can reduce the feelings of being overwhelmed that often accompany high-pressure situations. Utilizing tools such as the Eisenhower Matrix to categorize tasks based on urgency and importance can help you focus on high-priority activities and delegate or defer less critical ones. This structured approach to time management enhances productivity and provides a sense of control, mitigating the stress associated with looming deadlines and multiple responsibilities.

Building a robust support system is another crucial aspect of emotional regulation (Evans, 2021).[2] Surrounding yourself with trusted colleagues, mentors, or friends who can offer advice, perspective, and encouragement can be invaluable. These individuals can provide a sounding board for your concerns, helping you process your emotions and gain clarity. Additionally, seeking professional support from coaches or therapists can offer strategies tailored to your needs, further enhancing your ability to manage emotions under pressure. A robust support system provides practical assistance and emotional resilience, enabling you to navigate stressful situations with greater confidence and composure.

Lastly, physical well-being is intrinsically linked to emotional regulation. Regular exercise, a balanced diet, and sufficient sleep are fundamental to maintaining overall health and reducing stress. Physical activity, in particular, releases endorphins, which are natural mood elevators, helping to alleviate anxiety and improve your emotional state. Ensuring your physical health provides a strong foundation for managing your emotions effectively, especially in high-pressure environments. Integrating these practices into your daily routine can build resilience and enhance your capacity to handle stress and pressure with poise.

Building Empathy and Understanding Others

Empathy, a cornerstone of emotional intelligence, is the ability to recognize and understand the emotions of others. It is indispensable for effective leadership (Johnson, 2023).[3] As a manager, practicing empathy involves more than just acknowledging the feelings of your team members; it requires active listening and perspective-taking to connect with them genuinely. This skill fosters trust and creates a supportive work environment where team members feel valued and understood. By tuning into the emotional states of your colleagues, you can better navigate interpersonal dynamics, making informed decisions that benefit both the individual and the team.

To understand empathy's significance in management, consider its role in recognizing and understanding the emotions of others. Empathy enables you to perceive the underlying emotions driving a team member's behavior, allowing you to respond in a way that addresses their needs and concerns. This understanding builds trust and rapport, essential components of a cohesive team. When team members trust their manager, they are more likely to communicate openly, collaborate effectively, and commit to their work. Trust, once established, becomes the bedrock upon which productive and harmonious teams are built.

Several techniques can enhance your empathetic skills (Roberts, 2020).[4] Active listening is paramount; it involves fully engaging with the speaker, reflecting on their words, and validating their feelings. This technique shows that you value their perspective, fostering a sense of belonging and respect. Perspective-taking, another vital method, requires you to step into the shoes of others and consider their viewpoints and experiences. This practice broadens your understanding of their challenges and motivations, enabling you to respond with greater compassion and insight. Together, these techniques create a robust framework for empathetic leadership.

The benefits of empathy in the workplace extend to various facets of team dynamics. Empathy enhances team collaboration by fostering an environment where members feel safe to express their ideas and concerns. This open communication reduces conflicts and misunderstandings, promoting a more cohesive and efficient team. Additionally, empathy improves employee satisfaction and retention. When team members feel understood and supported, they are more likely to be engaged and committed to their roles, reducing turnover and enhancing overall productivity. The ripple effects of empathetic leadership can transform the workplace culture, making it more inclusive and supportive.

> "People don't leave jobs; they leave managers,"
> — Marcus Buckingham

Practical examples of empathetic leadership abound. Imagine a team member going through a personal challenge, such as a family illness. An empathetic manager would take the time to listen to the individual's concerns, offering support and flexibility to accommodate their needs. This might involve adjusting deadlines, providing additional resources, or simply being available for a conversation. Such actions demonstrate genuine concern, strengthening the manager's and team members' bond.

Empathy is not merely an abstract concept but a practical tool significantly impacting leadership effectiveness. By recognizing and understanding the emotions of others, building trust and rapport, and employing techniques like active listening and perspective-taking, you can enhance team collaboration, reduce conflicts, and improve employee satisfaction. Practical examples of empathetic leadership, such as empathetically supporting team members through personal challenges and resolving disputes, illustrate how these principles can be applied in real-world scenarios. As you cultivate empathy, you will find that it transforms your approach to leadership and enriches your interactions, creating a more positive and productive work environment.

Example: Addressing an Issue with Emotional Intelligence

Consider how a manager might handle an employee's repeated tardiness:

Without Emotional Intelligence: "John, you've been late several times this week. This is unacceptable, and if it continues, there will be consequences. We need you to be on time, or it will negatively affect your performance reviews."

This approach is purely disciplinary. It focuses on the problem without considering the employee's situation, which could make them defensive and harm the working relationship.

With Emotional Intelligence: "John, I've noticed you've been late a few times this week, and I wanted to check in with you. Is everything okay? I understand things outside of work can affect your schedule, and I'd like to find a solution together. How can I help you arrive on time?"

Using Emotional Intelligence to Resolve Conflicts

Workplace conflicts are inevitable in team dynamics, often stemming from differing perspectives, values, and interests. Emotions play a significant role in these conflicts, with the potential to either escalate tensions or aid in their resolution. Recognizing the emotional factors involved is essential for effective management.

Triggers such as perceived slights, unmet expectations, or competitive pressures can spark conflicts if not addressed. By identifying these triggers early, you can anticipate potential issues and resolve underlying tensions before they escalate. Equally important is being aware of everyone's emotional state. This awareness allows you to gauge the intensity of the emotions at play and adjust your approach to de-escalate the situation effectively.

Leveraging emotional intelligence in conflict resolution involves several strategic techniques, one of which is active listening, as mentioned earlier. Staying calm and composed during heated discussions is another critical strategy. Your demeanor sets the tone for the interaction, and maintaining poise helps keep the conversation constructive. As mentioned above, deep breathing techniques or mental reframing will help, ensuring that you remain focused on resolving the issue rather than reacting to provocations.

The benefits of resolving conflicts with emotional intelligence are manifold. Such an approach strengthens team relationships by fostering a culture of trust and mutual respect. Additionally, emotionally intelligent conflict resolution promotes a supportive work environment where issues can be addressed transparently and constructively. This openness enhances morale and encourages innovation and productivity, as team members feel safe to express their ideas and concerns without fear of retribution.

Real-life examples illuminate the practical application of these principles. Consider a manager mediating a dispute between team members with differing opinions on a project strategy. By actively listening to each party and acknowledging their valid points, the manager can facilitate a dialogue to find common ground. For instance, recognizing that both parties ultimately seek the project's success can shift the conversation from conflict to collaboration. Another example involves addressing a conflict between departments over resource allocation. A manager who stays composed and uses emotional intelligence to understand each department's priorities can broker a solution that respects both parties' needs, fostering interdepartmental cooperation and goodwill.

In conclusion, integrating emotional intelligence into conflict resolution transforms potentially divisive situations into opportunities for growth and unity. By understanding the emotional dynamics at play, employing strategic techniques to manage these emotions, and fostering a culture of openness and respect, you can navigate conflicts effectively, enhancing team cohesion and productivity. As we transition to the next chapter, we will explore the principles and practices of ethical leadership, examining how integrity and transparency can further strengthen your role as a leader.

Downloadable Resources

To give you a bit of extra help with what we've covered in this chapter, you'll find the following resources at the end of Chapter 15:

a. Emotional Intelligence EQ – A simple personality test for self-awareness.

b. Managers Journal – A handy journal to reflect on your day and plan the next.

Ethical Leadership

During a particularly challenging financial quarter, the CEO of a growing tech startup faced a dilemma that tested the core of her ethical principles. Investors were becoming impatient, pushing for swift and profitable results, even if it meant compromising the company's values. Despite the pressure, she remained steadfast, refusing to sacrifice integrity for short-term gains. Instead, she prioritized ethical practices, transparently communicating the company's challenges and strategies to her team and stakeholders. While her decision was initially met with skepticism, it ultimately earned her immense respect and trust, solidifying her reputation as a moral leader. This example highlights ethical leadership's critical role in navigating modern business's complexities.

Ethical leadership is defined by consistently applying integrity, fairness, and moral principles in decision-making and interactions. It goes beyond simply adhering to rules or guidelines, embodying a genuine commitment to doing what is right for the common good, even at a personal or financial cost. Acting with integrity and fairness forms the foundation of ethical leadership. This involves honesty, transparency, and equitability in all dealings, ensuring a solid moral compass guides every decision and action. Ethical leaders treat all team members with equal respect and consideration, regardless of their role or status.

Leading by example is another cornerstone of ethical leadership. Leaders who consistently demonstrate ethical behavior set a powerful standard for their teams. Through their actions, decisions, and interactions, they model the importance of integrity, creating a culture where ethical conduct is valued and emulated. This approach influences every aspect of leadership, from handling conflicts and making decisions to how leaders communicate and build relationships. By living out their values, ethical leaders inspire their teams to uphold the same standards, fostering a cohesive and principled organizational culture.

Transparency is another key principle that guides ethical leaders—being transparent means openly sharing the rationale behind decisions, including challenges, considerations, and potential impacts. This openness builds trust and inclusivity, helping team members feel informed and valued. Accountability is equally important. Ethical leaders take ownership of their actions, acknowledge mistakes, and use them as learning opportunities. They also hold their teams accountable, ensuring that ethical standards are upheld consistently. Treating all team members with respect, equity, and dignity further reinforces the commitment to creating an inclusive environment where diversity is embraced and everyone can thrive.

The influence of ethical leadership on team trust is profound. Ethical behavior fosters mutual respect, giving team members the confidence that their leader's actions are guided by integrity and fairness. This trust encourages open communication, allowing team members to share ideas, concerns, and feedback in an environment where they feel respected and valued. Leaders cultivate trust and loyalty through consistent ethical behavior, resulting in stronger, more cohesive, and productive teams.

> "The supreme quality of leadership is unquestionably integrity. Without it, no real success is possible."
> – Dwight D. Eisenhower

I remember a pivotal moment in my management career when our company discussed a significant price increase—well above what customers were used to. The potential financial gains were obvious, but I couldn't shake the feeling that it would negatively impact our loyal customers and put our frontline staff, like Sarah and Tom, in a tough position. I knew they'd be the ones handling calls and facing questions without much of an explanation to give for such a sharp increase.

It was one of those times when I felt it was crucial to speak up. I raised my concerns with the leadership team, stressing the importance of transparency and fairness. I suggested a more moderate price adjustment, something Sarah, Tom, and the rest of the team could confidently explain to customers without feeling caught in the middle. I emphasized that maintaining trust with our customers and sparing our staff from avoidable conflict would be worth much more in the long run than a short-term financial bump.

Ultimately, the company decided to go with the adjusted pricing strategy. It wasn't an easy decision for anyone, but it felt right. Seeing Sarah and Tom able to handle customer calls with confidence and honesty reinforced how prioritizing transparency and fairness helped us keep our customers' trust. It also showed our team that we valued their relationships with those customers just as much as our bottom line. This experience taught me how essential ethical leadership is, no matter your position. Standing up for what's fair can impact team morale and customer loyalty even without being at the top.

Reflection Exercise: Assessing Ethical Leadership in Your Role

Take a moment to reflect on your recent decisions and actions as a leader. Consider whether you have consistently acted with integrity and fairness and led by example in promoting ethical behavior. Identify specific instances where you demonstrated transparency and accountability, and think about how these actions impacted your team's trust and morale. Use these reflections to identify areas to strengthen your ethical leadership practices further.

By integrating the principles of ethical leadership into your daily practices, you can foster a culture of trust, respect, and accountability, ultimately leading to more cohesive and successful teams. The journey towards ethical leadership is continuous, requiring ongoing reflection, commitment, and action.

Making Ethical Decisions

Navigating ethical choices during decision-making often demands a robust and structured framework. The Utilitarian Approach, focused on the greatest good for the most significant number, is one of the primary ethical decision-making models (Evans, 2021).[1] This approach evaluates the consequences of actions, aiming to maximize overall happiness and minimize harm. For instance, when deciding on budget cuts, a manager using the Utilitarian Approach would weigh the potential benefits and detriments to all stakeholders, striving to choose the option that yields the most favorable outcomes for the majority. While seemingly straightforward, this approach demands a meticulous balancing of competing interests and outcomes, often requiring a granular analysis of potential impacts.

The Rights Approach, another vital framework, emphasizes protecting and respecting individual rights (Martinez, 2022).[2] This model is grounded in the belief that certain rights—such as the right to privacy, freedom of speech, and fair treatment—are inviolable and must be upheld irrespective of the consequences. This approach mandates that decisions respect all individuals' inherent dignity and rights. For example, in implementing new surveillance measures within an organization, a manager guided by the Rights Approach would ensure that employees' privacy rights are not unduly compromised, balancing the need for security with respect for personal boundaries.

The Fairness or Justice Approach complements these models and prioritizes equitable treatment and fairness in decision-making (Harris, 2021).[3] This framework is particularly pertinent in resource allocation, promotions, and disciplinary actions. The Fairness Approach demands that decisions are impartial and grounded in principles of justice, ensuring that all individuals are treated equitably. For instance, when evaluating candidates for a promotion, a manager adhering to this approach would base their decision on merit, performance, and qualifications, eschewing any form of favoritism or bias.

The ethical decision-making process unfolds through deliberate steps to ensure thorough evaluation and moral action (Roberts, 2020).[4] The first step involves identifying the ethical issues and recognizing the moral dimensions of the decision and the stakeholders affected. This requires a keen awareness of the broader implications of each choice beyond immediate practical considerations. Next, the consequences of various actions must be meticulously considered, weighing potential benefits and harms. This step often involves scenario planning and impact analysis, envisioning the ripple effects of each possible decision. Evaluation of alternatives based on ethical principles follows, employing the earlier frameworks to scrutinize each option. This stage demands a nuanced understanding of ethical theories and their application to real-world dilemmas, ensuring that choices align with moral values and standards. The decision is made once alternatives have been evaluated and action is taken, guided by a commitment to ethical principles. This step necessitates decisiveness and courage, as ethical decisions often involve navigating complex, multifaceted challenges.

However, making ethical decisions is fraught with challenges. Conflicts of interest frequently arise where personal or organizational interests clash with ethical imperatives. For instance, a manager might face a dilemma when selecting a vendor, torn between choosing a longtime business associate and a more qualified but less familiar company. Pressure to meet business targets further complicates ethical decision-making. The relentless pursuit of financial goals can sometimes obscure ethical considerations, compelling managers to prioritize short-term gains over long-term integrity.

I remember facing a similar ethical dilemma early in my career as a manager. I was responsible for selecting a vendor for a significant project, and one of the options was a long-time business associate—someone I had a good relationship with and trusted. On the other hand, another company was less familiar to me, but they were more qualified for the job. It wasn't an easy decision. The pressure to maintain the business relationship with my associate was intense, and it would have been easy to justify awarding them the contract. But after careful consideration, I knew that the fair and ethical choice was to go with the more qualified vendor, even if it meant straining that personal connection. In the end, prioritizing integrity over convenience helped foster a sense of trust and transparency within the organization. It was a difficult choice, but sticking to ethical principles allowed me to make the right decision, and the long-term benefits far outweighed the short-term discomfort.

Another example involves navigating ethical issues in performance evaluations. A manager discovered that a high-performing employee had engaged in unethical behavior. The manager opted for a transparent approach to balance recognizing the employee's contributions with the imperative to address misconduct. They conducted a thorough investigation, provided the employee an opportunity to explain, and implemented corrective measures while reinforcing ethical standards. This decision addressed the immediate issue and reinforced the organization's commitment to ethical conduct, setting a precedent for future evaluations.

Ethical decision-making, while complex, is navigable through structured frameworks and moral action. Managers can systematically evaluate ethical dilemmas by employing models such as the Utilitarian, Rights, and Fairness Approaches, balancing competing interests and upholding moral integrity. The step-by-step process of identifying ethical issues, considering consequences, evaluating alternatives, and taking moral action ensures that decisions are ethically sound and practically viable. However, the challenges of conflicts of interest and business pressures underscore the need for vigilance and courage in ethical decision-making. Real-life scenarios provide concrete illustrations of these principles in action, demonstrating how ethical decisions can be made and upheld in the face of complex and competing demands.

Building an Ethical Workplace Culture

The bedrock of long-term success is often found in establishing an ethical workplace culture. This foundation is not merely a collection of lofty ideals but a pragmatic necessity that profoundly influences every facet of an organization, from employee satisfaction to legal compliance. An ethical culture enhances employee satisfaction and retention by fostering an environment where individuals feel respected, valued, and aligned with the organization's values. Employees who perceive that their organization prioritizes ethical conduct are likelier to remain engaged and committed, reducing turnover rates and enhancing overall productivity. Furthermore, a moral culture mitigates the risk of legal issues, as adherence to ethical standards often aligns with legal requirements, safeguarding the organization against potential legal ramifications.

Promoting ethical behavior within an organization requires deliberate and strategic efforts. One of the most effective methods is developing a clear code of ethics. This document serves as a guiding framework, outlining the organization's values, principles, and expectations for behavior. It provides employees with a roadmap for ethical conduct, clarifying acceptable and unacceptable behavior. Regular communication and reinforcement of this code are crucial, ensuring it remains a living document rather than a forgotten policy.

Additionally, regular ethics training is essential for instilling and reinforcing ethical behavior. These training sessions should be interactive and scenario-based, allowing employees to engage with real-world ethical dilemmas and practice ethical decision-making. Regular training educates employees about the organization's ethical standards and reinforces the importance of ethical conduct in their daily work.

The role of leadership in shaping and reinforcing an ethical culture cannot be overstated. Leaders set the tone for the entire organization, and their actions and behaviors serve as models for employees to emulate. Leading by example is paramount; when leaders consistently demonstrate ethical behavior, they signal to the entire organization that ethics are a priority. This includes making decisions transparently, taking responsibility for their actions, and treating all employees fairly and respectfully. Recognizing and rewarding ethical behavior further reinforces the importance of ethics within the organization. This can be achieved through formal recognition programs, such as awards for ethical conduct, or informal acknowledgments, such as public praise during team meetings. By celebrating ethical behavior, leaders create a culture where ethics are valued and upheld.

Various tools and resources can support the cultivation of an ethical culture. Ethical audits, for example, provide a comprehensive assessment of the organization's ethical practices, identifying areas of strength and opportunities for improvement. These audits involve reviewing policies, procedures, and practices to ensure alignment with ethical standards. Additionally, establishing ethics committees or councils can provide ongoing oversight and guidance on ethical matters. These committees, composed of employees from various levels and departments, serve as a forum for discussing ethical issues, offering recommendations, and ensuring that ethical considerations are integrated into decision-making processes. Another valuable tool is the implementation of anonymous reporting systems, which allow employees to report unethical behavior without fear of retribution. These systems can include hotlines, online reporting platforms, or suggestion boxes, providing employees multiple avenues to voice their concerns.

In conclusion, building an ethical workplace culture is a multifaceted effort that relies on clear guidelines, continuous education, and strong leadership.

As we transition to the next chapter, we'll delve into the art of navigating difficult conversations. Building on the principles of ethical leadership, we'll explore how to approach sensitive discussions with empathy, clarity, and confidence, ensuring that even the toughest conversations can lead to positive outcomes for both individuals and the team.

Mastering Difficult Conversations

Imagine a scenario on a busy construction site where Jason, a project manager, needs to deliver difficult feedback to a crew member who isn't meeting expectations. The stakes are high; the project's success depends on every team member pulling their weight. As Jason prepares for the conversation, he reflects on past instances where feedback was taken the wrong way or led to tension among the team. The challenge isn't just to address the issue—it's to communicate to encourage improvement, maintain respect, and strengthen trust. This chapter explores the art of delivering constructive feedback, a vital skill that, when used effectively, turns potential conflict into an opportunity for growth and team cohesion.

Delivering Constructive Feedback

Constructive feedback is a cornerstone of effective management, driving personal and team growth. Its significance lies in its ability to enhance performance and development by providing individuals with the guidance they need to refine their skills and behaviors. For example, if a team member consistently misses deadlines, constructive feedback can pinpoint the issue and offer actionable advice, such as improving time management strategies. This ongoing feedback and refinement process is vital for fostering progress at individual and team levels.

In addition to promoting growth, constructive feedback is crucial in building trust and encouraging open communication within a team. Feedback delivered with empathy and clarity shows team members that their development is valued. This creates a culture of openness, where individuals feel safe sharing concerns and seeking guidance. Trust, once established, becomes a key driver of team cohesion and productivity. Furthermore, addressing issues through timely and effective feedback prevents minor problems from escalating into significant challenges. By resolving concerns early, managers can maintain harmony within the team and ensure a productive and supportive work environment.

A structured approach to delivering feedback ensures that it is clear, actionable, and impactful. One such framework is the Situation-Behavior-Impact (SBI) model, which outlines feedback in three parts: Situation, Behavior, and Impact. First, the Situation component involves describing the specific time and place of the incident, providing context to ground the feedback in reality. For example, "During last Tuesday's team meeting, you interrupted your colleague several times." Next, the Behavior component states the actions being addressed, focusing on observable actions rather than personal attributes. "You spoke over them and didn't let them finish their thoughts." Finally, the Impact component explains how the behavior affects others or the organization. "This disrupted the meeting flow and made your colleague feel disrespected." By providing specific examples and objective observations, this model minimizes misunderstandings and ensures that feedback is constructive and actionable (Evans, 2021).[1]

Another popular technique is the Feedback Sandwich, which structures feedback to cushion negative observations between positive remarks. This method begins with praise, followed by constructive criticism, and concludes with additional positive feedback. For example, "Your recent project presentation was very engaging and well-researched. However, there were a few instances where the data was not as clear as it could have been. Overall, your ability to captivate the audience was impressive, and with more clarity in your data, it will be exceptional." This approach aims to soften the impact of negative feedback, making it more palatable and encouraging a positive reception. However, it is essential to ensure that the positive feedback is genuine and relevant, as insincere praise can undermine the effectiveness of the input.

Setting specific, measurable, achievable, relevant, and time-bound (SMART) goals is another critical aspect of delivering constructive feedback. Providing feedback that includes clear, actionable steps ensures that team members know precisely what is expected of them and how to achieve it. For instance, if a team member needs to improve their presentation skills, a SMART goal might be, "Enhance presentation skills by attending a public speaking workshop within the next month and practicing with the team weekly." This goal is specific (enhance presentation skills), measurable (attend a workshop and practice weekly), achievable (realistic given the resources), relevant (aligned with job responsibilities), and time-bound (within the next month). By setting SMART goals, managers provide a clear roadmap for improvement, facilitating personal and professional development (Roberts, 2020).[2]

The timing and setting of feedback delivery are crucial for its effectiveness. Choosing a private and comfortable setting ensures that the recipient feels safe and respected, free from the pressure or embarrassment of public scrutiny. Feedback should be timely and delivered as soon as possible after the observed behavior, ensuring that the details are fresh and relevant. However, ensuring that the feedback is considered and well-prepared is equally important, and avoiding impulsive or emotionally charged responses is equally important. Avoiding high-stress moments or public settings further enhances the receptivity of the feedback, allowing for a more constructive and open dialogue.

Reflective Exercise: Practicing the SBI Model

Reflect on a recent situation where you needed to deliver constructive feedback. Consider the following prompts:

- What was the specific situation, and how did it unfold?

- What behavior did you observe, and how did it impact the team or project?

- How did you deliver the feedback, and what was the outcome?

- What worked well, and what could have been improved?

Using the SBI model, rewrite your feedback, ensuring each component is clearly articulated. Practice this revised feedback with a colleague or mentor, and reflect on the differences in response and effectiveness. This exercise will help refine your feedback delivery skills, enhancing your ability to provide constructive and impactful feedback.

By mastering the art of delivering constructive feedback, you can transform challenging conversations into opportunities for growth and development. This skill enhances individual performance and fosters a culture of trust and openness, driving team cohesion and success. You will find that even the most difficult conversations can be navigated with confidence and empathy as you refine your feedback techniques.

Responsible Delegation and Empowerment

Delegation, a critical skill for any manager, involves the strategic distribution of tasks to team members, allowing managers to focus on higher-level strategic activities while concurrently aiding in the professional development of their subordinates. By effectively delegating tasks, managers alleviate their workload and foster an environment where team members can hone their skills, gain confidence, and take on greater responsibilities. This balance between managerial oversight and team autonomy is pivotal for organizational success. Consider the scenario where a manager, overwhelmed by a myriad of tasks, decides to delegate the oversight of a routine project to a capable team member. This act empowers the team members and enables the manager to concentrate on more strategic initiatives.

Successful delegation begins with identifying tasks suitable for delegation. Not all tasks are created equal; some require the manager's direct oversight, while others are prime candidates for delegation. Routine, time-consuming tasks, or those that offer developmental opportunities for team members, are ideal for delegation. Managers can determine which responsibilities can be entrusted to others by categorizing tasks based on their complexity and importance. For instance, administrative duties, data analysis, or preliminary research tasks can often be delegated, freeing up the manager's time for strategic planning and decision-making.

Once suitable tasks are identified, matching them to team members' strengths is crucial. This alignment ensures that tasks are assigned to individuals best equipped to handle them based on their skills, experience, and professional development goals. Understanding each team member's competencies and aspirations allows for more informed and effective delegation. For example, suppose a team member excels in data analysis. In that case, assigning them a complex data-driven project leverages their strengths and allows them to develop their expertise further.

Providing clear instructions and ensuring accountability through regular check-ins form the backbone of responsible delegation. These check-ins should be structured yet flexible, allowing open communication and feedback. For instance, a manager might schedule bi-weekly meetings to review progress, offer guidance, and address any challenges the team members may encounter.

Responsible delegation entails more than just assigning tasks; it involves a thoughtful and strategic approach. Matching tasks with team members' skills is paramount. This alignment ensures tasks are completed efficiently and contributes to the team member's professional growth. Providing the necessary resources and support is equally critical. This might involve offering access to relevant tools, training, or mentorship, ensuring the team member is well-equipped to succeed. For example, delegating a project requiring specialized software might necessitate providing the team members access to the software and any necessary training or support.

A structured approach to delegating tasks responsibly involves several key steps. Firstly, clearly defining the task and expectations is essential. This includes outlining the task's objectives, expected outcomes, and specific requirements or constraints. Setting deadlines and milestones further ensures that the task stays on track and progress can be monitored. These deadlines should be realistic and achievable, providing a clear timeline for task completion. Monitoring progress and providing feedback throughout the task's duration is crucial.

When executed responsibly, delegation can be a powerful tool for empowering team members and promoting their growth. Encouraging autonomy and decision-making allows team members to take ownership of their tasks, fostering a sense of responsibility and accountability. Providing opportunities for skill development further enhances this empowerment. This might involve assigning tasks that challenge team members to step out of their comfort zones and develop new competencies. For instance, delegating a leadership role in a project to a junior team member can provide them with valuable experience and boost their confidence.

I've seen firsthand the power of effective delegation in my management career. I remember one particular project where I was stretched thin across multiple responsibilities. Instead of handling every detail myself, I delegated critical tasks to my team. I assigned specific roles to individuals I trusted, like Ben and Priya, giving them ownership over crucial parts of the project. This allowed me to focus on the bigger picture while letting them step up and showcase their skills.

One standout example was when I entrusted Priya, a junior team member, with leading a smaller project within a much larger initiative. At first, she was nervous and unsure if she was ready for the responsibility. I could see her hesitation, so I made it clear that I believed in her abilities and was there to support her if needed. As the project progressed, Priya started handling challenges with growing confidence. She took on each task with determination, and it was rewarding to watch her flourish in a leadership role for the first time.

By the project's end, we had achieved our goals, and Priya had grown immensely. She went on to take up even more leadership responsibilities in future projects, and the experience showed me the value of thoughtful delegation. It lightened my workload and allowed my team members to develop and succeed. Watching them grow through the process reminded them that delegation isn't just about efficiency—it's about empowering others to reach their potential.

When done effectively, responsible delegation can transform management, creating a culture of empowerment and fostering growth within the team.

Decision-Making Skills

Imagine standing at the helm of a ship, navigating through turbulent waters. Each wave represents a decision, and each current has a potential consequence. Success depends on having clear navigation tools and a solid strategy. Decision-making, much like steering that vessel, requires a well-defined framework to manage the complexities and uncertainties of leadership effectively. Structured frameworks provide a systematic approach to evaluating options, considering consequences, and making informed choices, helping to reduce uncertainty and increase the chances of a successful outcome.

Several decision-making models have garnered widespread acclaim for their efficacy in business settings. The Rational Decision-Making Model, the Bounded Rationality Model, and the Vroom-Yetton Decision Model each offer unique approaches tailored to different scenarios (Garcia, 2021).[1] These frameworks facilitate a structured and logical process, ensuring that decisions are not merely reactive but are grounded in thorough analysis and consideration. The benefits of using such frameworks are manifold. They enhance objectivity by minimizing biases, providing a clear decision-making roadmap, and enabling managers to make informed, consistent, and transparent decisions.

The Rational Decision-Making Model is a prime example of a logical and systematic approach to decision-making. This model unfolds through several structured steps, starting with identifying the problem. Recognizing the core issue is crucial because a misdiagnosis can derail the entire process. Once the problem is clearly defined, the next step is to generate alternative solutions, encouraging creative thinking and exploring multiple potential courses of action. After generating alternatives, the next crucial step is to evaluate these options by analyzing their pros and cons, considering factors like feasibility, risks, and alignment with organizational goals. Finally, the best option is selected based on a comprehensive assessment of the available information. This logical sequence ensures that decisions are data-driven and thoroughly considered, minimizing the chances of errors and incorrect assumptions.

However, no model is without its limitations. While objective and thorough, the Rational Decision-Making Model requires extensive information and time (Taylor, 2021).[2] This can be a drawback in fast-paced environments where decisions must be made swiftly. Additionally, its emphasis on data and logic may limit risk-taking and innovation. The Rational Decision-Making Model excels in structured environments with ample data and time, making it ideal for strategic planning and complex problem-solving.

The practical application of these models in managerial scenarios illuminates their utility. Consider a situation where a company faces a budget shortfall. Using the Rational Decision-Making Model, a manager would begin by identifying the core issue—such as overspending or revenue shortfall—and then generate alternative solutions like cost-cutting measures or revenue enhancement strategies.

In essence, decision-making frameworks provide a structured and systematic approach to navigating the complexities of managerial decisions. By understanding and applying these models, you can enhance your decision-making capabilities, ensuring that your choices are informed, objective, and aligned with organizational goals. It would be beneficial to explore all three models. This book focuses on The Rational Decision-Making Model.

Avoiding Decision-Making Paralysis

Decision-making paralysis is a common challenge in managerial settings. It often appears as an inability to make timely decisions due to overwhelming choices or fear of making the wrong move. This paralysis, marked by procrastination and over-analysis, can significantly hinder productivity and progress. The fear of making an incorrect decision is often amplified in high-stakes environments, making any choice seem impossible. Understanding the underlying causes of this paralysis is the first step to overcoming it, enabling the use of more targeted and effective strategies.

Decision making can be turbulent

Several techniques can help break the cycle of indecision. Setting deadlines is an effective way to combat decision-making paralysis by creating urgency and pushing the process forward. Deadlines prevent over-analysis by forcing you to focus on the critical factors, prioritize information, and make a decision. Another strategy is breaking down significant decisions into smaller, manageable steps, which reduces cognitive load and makes the process less overwhelming. For example, rather than deciding on an entire marketing strategy at once, you could start by defining the target audience and then determine the messaging and channels. It's also essential to prioritize decisions based on their impact. Not all decisions carry the same weight—focusing on high-impact ones first ensures your efforts are spent on what matters most, while less critical decisions can be postponed or delegated.

Building confidence in your decision-making abilities is essential for overcoming paralysis. Reflecting on past successful decisions can instill a sense of competence and assurance. By analyzing what worked well in previous scenarios, you can identify patterns and strategies that can be applied to current decisions. This reflection boosts confidence and provides valuable insights into your decision-making strengths. Seeking input and validation from trusted colleagues is another effective way to enhance confidence. Colleagues can offer different perspectives, identify potential blind spots, and provide reassurance, making the decision-making process more collaborative and less isolating.

I used to suffer from severe analysis paralysis, often avoiding tough decisions for fear of making the wrong call. One pivotal moment was during a critical product launch when the pressure of choosing the right strategy left me completely stuck. Realizing that inaction would do more harm than a wrong choice, I changed my approach.

I set a firm deadline, which forced me to prioritize what mattered. Breaking the decision into smaller, manageable steps helped ease the overwhelm. I focused on the target audience and worked through messaging and marketing channels. Seeking input from my team also proved invaluable—they offered perspectives I hadn't considered, which boosted my confidence.

Ultimately, the product launch went smoothly, and the experience taught me the power of structured decision-making. By breaking tasks down and collaborating with others, I learned to make timely decisions without getting bogged down in unnecessary details. This approach helped me grow as a leader and break free from analysis paralysis for good.

Overcoming decision-making paralysis requires a multifaceted approach that addresses both the psychological and practical aspects of decision-making. The above strategies alleviate the paralysis and enhance the overall decision-making process, enabling you to make timely, informed, and confident choices.

> **You don't have to see the whole staircase, just take the first step.**
> – Martin Luther King Jr

Balancing Data and Intuition

Navigating the complexity between data and intuition is challenging for all (Garcia, 2023).[3] The utility of data lies in its ability to enhance objectivity, stripping away the biases and assumptions that often cloud human judgment. By providing concrete insights and trends, data allows you to ground your decisions in empirical evidence. For instance, a sales manager relying on quarterly sales reports can identify consumer behavior patterns, thus making informed decisions about inventory and marketing strategies. Data-driven insights are particularly valuable in environments where precision and accuracy are critical, offering a reliable foundation for building strategic plans.

However, there are scenarios where data alone may be insufficient, and intuition becomes an invaluable asset. There often isn't time to sift through copious amounts of data in high-pressure situations demanding rapid decision-making, such as crisis management or urgent client negotiations. Here, intuition, drawn from years of experience and pattern recognition, plays a pivotal role. A seasoned manager, for example, might rely on their gut feeling to make a swift decision during a financial downturn, leveraging their deep understanding of market dynamics. Similarly, intuition can guide you through the uncertainty in ambiguous scenarios where data is sparse or inconclusive, drawing upon your accumulated knowledge and insights.

The challenge, however, lies in striking a balance between data and intuition, integrating the empirical with the experiential. One practical approach is to use data to inform your intuitive judgments, creating a synergistic relationship between the two. Start by gathering and analyzing relevant data to provide a factual basis for your decisions. Once you have this foundation, allow your intuition to interpret the data, considering the nuances and context that numbers alone cannot capture. Cross-checking your intuitive decisions with available data can further enhance accuracy and reliability. For instance, if your intuition suggests a particular market strategy, validate it by examining customer feedback and market trends to ensure alignment with empirical evidence.

As a trainer, I often relied on intuition, but this wasn't enough when filling places for a free work placement program I oversaw. Despite the value of the training, we struggled with low enrollments, and I couldn't figure out why.

I brought in a data-savvy team member, and together, we analyzed past trends and feedback. The data showed that timing and communication were vital issues—managers hesitated to release employees for training, and our outreach wasn't well-timed. With this insight, we adjusted our messaging and promotional strategy to address managers' concerns and target the correct times to promote the program.

As a result, enrollments improved significantly, and I learned the importance of blending data-driven insights with intuition to make informed decisions.

Reflective Exercise: Balancing Data and Intuition in Decision-Making

Reflect on a recent decision where you relied primarily on data or intuition. Consider the following prompts:

- How did data inform your decision, and what insights did it provide?

- In what ways did your intuition play a role, and how did it influence the outcome?

- How might integrating data and intuition have enhanced the decision-making process?

Write down your reflections and identify opportunities to balance data and intuition in future decisions. This exercise will help you develop a nuanced decision-making approach, leveraging empirical evidence and experiential insights to navigate complex managerial challenges.

Evaluating Outcomes and Learning from Mistakes

Evaluating decision outcomes is not merely a procedural step but a crucial practice that underpins effective management (Johnson, 2024).[4] Through this evaluative lens, you can discern your decisions' efficacy, identifying successes and areas for improvement. This reflective process is essential for learning from your triumphs and failures, enabling you to adjust your strategies and refine your decision-making processes for the future. By systematically assessing outcomes, you can ensure that your decisions align with organizational goals and contribute to sustained growth and development.

To assess the effectiveness of your decisions, employing various techniques can provide a comprehensive perspective. Key Performance Indicators (KPIs) serve as quantifiable metrics that gauge the success of your actions against predefined goals. For instance, if your decision aimed to enhance customer satisfaction, relevant KPIs might include customer feedback scores, repeat purchase rates, or net promoter scores. These metrics offer tangible evidence of your decision's impact, allowing you to make necessary data-driven adjustments. Another valuable technique is the post-implementation review, which thoroughly examines the decision's outcomes after execution. This review process encourages you to reflect on what worked well, what didn't, and why. By engaging in candid discussions with your team, you can uncover insights that might not be immediately apparent, fostering a culture of transparency and continuous improvement.

Learning from mistakes is a pivotal aspect of managerial growth. Though often perceived negatively, mistakes are invaluable learning opportunities that can catalyze personal and organizational development. Conducting a thorough root-cause analysis is a critical step in this learning process. By delving into the underlying factors that contributed to the mistake, you can identify systemic issues, procedural gaps, or cognitive biases that must be addressed. This analysis should be objective and comprehensive, exploring direct and indirect causes. Implementing corrective actions and preventive measures based on your findings is equally essential. These actions might involve revising processes, enhancing training programs, or introducing new checks and balances. Encouraging a culture of continuous improvement ensures that lessons learned from mistakes are integrated into everyday practices, fostering resilience and adaptability within your team.

Consider the case of a tech company that faced a significant setback with a failed product launch. The company conducted an exhaustive root-cause analysis, which revealed that inadequate market research and rushed development timelines were primary contributors to the failure. In response, the company implemented robust market research protocols and restructured its development process to include more iterative testing and validation stages. This proactive approach rectified the immediate issues and strengthened the company's overall product development strategy, leading to more successful launches in the future. Another example involves a retail manager who encountered a poorly received promotional campaign. The manager analyzed customer feedback and sales data and identified that the campaign's messaging did not resonate with the target audience. The manager then collaborated with the marketing team to refine the messaging and timing of future promotions, resulting in significantly improved engagement and sales performance.

Evaluating outcomes and learning from mistakes are integral to effective decision-making. By systematically assessing the results of your decisions, you can glean valuable insights that inform future strategies and actions. Learning from successes and failures enables you to refine your approach, driving continuous personal and organizational growth.

Downloadable Resources

To complement this chapter, the following resources are available for download at the end of Chapter 15:

a. Decision-making rational – a logical and systematic approach to decision-making.

Building High-Performing Teams

Consider this: A promising startup, fresh from securing a significant round of funding, is preparing to scale its operations. The CEO, fully aware of the opportunities and challenges of rapid growth, knows that the foundation of success lies in building a high-performing team. The key to this effort isn't individual brilliance but the collective strength of a cohesive, trust-filled unit. In the diverse dynamics of a team, trust becomes the vital thread that binds individuals together, enhancing collaboration, reducing conflicts, and fostering an environment where innovation can thrive.

Trust is the cornerstone of strong team dynamics. Without it, misunderstandings, miscommunications, and conflicts can hinder productivity and stifle innovation. When trust is present, collaboration thrives as team members feel safe sharing ideas, voicing concerns, and engaging in honest dialogue. This openness fosters effective problem-solving, mutual respect, and a sense of camaraderie. Trust also helps to minimize conflicts by encouraging transparency and accountability. In a trusting environment, team members are more likely to approach disagreements constructively, give one another the benefit of the doubt, and work together to find solutions.

Practical team-building activities can effectively foster this indispensable trust. Trust falls, where one team member falls backward into the arms of their peers, symbolizes the literal and figurative act of placing one's faith in another. These exercises, while seemingly simplistic, have profound implications for team cohesion. They require team members to surrender control and trust their colleagues, reinforcing mutual reliance. Group problem-solving challenges, such as the "Perfect Square" exercise where blindfolded participants must form a square using only verbal instructions, further emphasize the importance of communication and cooperation. These activities compel team members to rely on each other's strengths and insights, fostering a more profound sense of unity and collaboration. Another engaging exercise is "Two Truths and a Lie," where participants share two factual statements and one falsehood about themselves. This activity introduces an element of fun and encourages team members to share personal stories, thereby humanizing each other and building interpersonal connections.

Regular team bonding sessions are essential for maintaining and deepening trust over time. Monthly team outings or social events allow team members to interact in a relaxed, informal setting, free from the pressures of work-related tasks. These outings range from casual dinners and game nights to adventurous activities like hiking or escape rooms. By stepping outside the confines of the office, team members can form more authentic connections and strengthen their interpersonal relationships. Regular "get-to-know-you" meetings, where team members share updates about their lives, interests, and experiences, further reinforce these bonds. These meetings can be structured or informal, but their purpose remains: to create opportunities for genuine interaction and foster a sense of belonging.

Creating a safe environment for vulnerability is essential for building trust. Encouraging team members to share personal experiences and challenges fosters an atmosphere of empathy and understanding. When individuals feel safe to express their vulnerabilities, they are more likely to trust their colleagues and engage in open, honest communication. This sense of vulnerability can be cultivated through structured activities like team reflection sessions, where members discuss their successes, failures, and lessons learned. Leading by example is crucial in this regard. When managers openly share their own vulnerabilities—whether it's a past mistake or a current challenge—they signal to their team that it is safe to do the same. This kind of transparency humanizes the manager and sets a powerful precedent for the entire team.

Reflective Exercise: Building Trust Through Vulnerability

Take a few moments to reflect on a recent instance where you felt vulnerable in a professional setting. Consider how you handled the situation and its impact on your relationships with your team members. Now, think about ways you can create opportunities for your team to share their vulnerabilities. Whether through structured activities or informal conversations, identify specific actions you can take to foster a more open, trust-filled environment.

By integrating trust-building exercises into your team's routine, you can cultivate an environment where collaboration thrives, conflicts are minimized, and innovation flourishes. Trust is not a static attribute but a dynamic quality that requires continuous nurturing and reinforcement.

You can build a high-performing team grounded in mutual respect and trust through deliberate actions and consistent effort.

Effective Collaboration Techniques

Effective collaboration is the foundation of any high-performing team and depends on several key principles. First, clear roles and responsibilities are essential. They provide each team member with a well-defined scope of work, ensuring everyone understands what is expected and how their contributions fit into the bigger picture. This clarity reduces confusion and overlap, fostering a more efficient and cohesive workflow. Open and transparent communication is equally important, as it allows information and ideas to flow freely, keeping everyone informed, aligned, and engaged. With transparent communication, misunderstandings are minimized, and collaboration becomes more seamless and productive.

Facilitating collaborative meetings requires careful planning and execution. Setting clear agendas and goals is the first step to ensuring that meetings are purposeful and focused. A compelling agenda outlines the topics to be discussed, the objectives of the meeting, and the expected outcomes, providing a roadmap that keeps discussions on track and prevents digressions. Encouraging equal participation from all members is also vital. This can be achieved by creating an inclusive environment where everyone feels comfortable sharing their ideas and perspectives. Techniques such as round-robin discussions, where each person has a chance to speak, or using a "talking stick" to manage turn-taking, can help ensure that all voices are heard. By fostering a culture of inclusivity, you can tap into your team's diverse insights and expertise, leading to more innovative solutions and better decision-making.

Leveraging collaborative tools and technologies can significantly enhance the efficiency and effectiveness of teamwork. Project management software like Trello and Asana provides a centralized platform for tracking tasks, deadlines, and progress, ensuring that everyone is on the same page and that nothing falls through the cracks. These tools often come with features like task assignments, progress tracking, and deadline reminders, which help streamline project management and foster accountability. Communication platforms like Slack and Microsoft Teams facilitate real-time communication and collaboration, allowing team members to instantly share updates, ask questions, and provide feedback. These platforms often integrate with other tools and apps, creating a seamless workflow that enhances productivity. Collaborative document tools like Google Docs and Microsoft SharePoint allow multiple users to work on the same document simultaneously, making it easy to create, edit, and review documents in real time. These tools save time and enhance the quality of collaborative work by enabling continuous feedback and iteration.

Encouraging cross-functional collaboration is another powerful strategy for fostering teamwork and innovation. Organizing cross-functional projects and teams brings together individuals with diverse skills, expertise, and perspectives, creating a rich tapestry of ideas and solutions. This diversity can lead to more creative and effective problem-solving as team members approach challenges from different angles and contribute unique insights. Creating opportunities for knowledge sharing and learning is also essential. This can be achieved through regular workshops, training sessions, and knowledge-sharing platforms, where team members can exchange ideas, share best practices, and learn from each other's experiences. By fostering a culture of continuous learning and collaboration, you can enhance the collective intelligence of your team and drive sustained innovation and growth.

I remember a time when several departments in the company I worked for seemed to operate in silos, even though they were all striving toward the same goal. Each team focused on their tasks without understanding how their work impacted other departments. To address this, I suggested that each department have its members write a simple one-sentence explanation of their role. This small exercise made a big difference—once everyone could see how their work connected, it helped foster better collaboration. For example, the sales department realized that slightly tweaking one of their processes could make things much easier for the client onboarding team. This simple change improved efficiency across departments and strengthened communication. We could work more effectively toward our common goal by encouraging this cross-departmental understanding.

Conflict Resolution Strategies

Understanding the nature of team conflicts is crucial for any manager aiming to cultivate a harmonious and productive work environment. Conflicts typically manifest in two primary forms: task conflicts and relationship conflicts. Task conflicts arise from differences in viewpoints and opinions regarding work-related tasks, such as project strategies, resource allocation, or deadlines. When managed constructively, these conflicts can stimulate creativity and lead to better decision-making by incorporating diverse perspectives. On the other hand, relationship conflicts are rooted in personal differences, emotional discord, or personality clashes, often resulting in tension and decreased team cohesion. While task conflicts can be beneficial if handled appropriately, relationship conflicts tend to be destructive, undermining trust and collaboration.

Additionally, conflicts can be categorized as constructive or destructive. Constructive conflicts, characterized by respectful dialogue and a focus on problem-solving, can enhance team understanding and innovation. Conversely, destructive conflicts involve personal attacks, defensiveness, and a communication breakdown, leading to a toxic work environment and reduced productivity.

As a manager, your role as a mediator in team conflicts is paramount. Remaining neutral and unbiased is essential for maintaining credibility and trust. When disputes arise, it is crucial to approach the situation without preconceived notions or favoritism. Encouraging both parties to express their viewpoints ensures that all voices are heard, fostering a balanced and inclusive dialogue. Helping parties find a mutually agreeable solution often involves guiding the conversation towards common goals and facilitating compromise. This might include brainstorming potential solutions, evaluating the pros and cons of each option, and collaboratively selecting the most viable course of action. Your ability to mediate effectively can transform conflicts into opportunities for growth and strengthened relationships.

Preventing conflicts before they arise is a proactive approach that can save time and resources. Setting clear expectations and guidelines establishes a common understanding of roles, responsibilities, and acceptable behaviors. This clarity reduces the likelihood of misunderstandings and misaligned expectations, common sources of conflict. Encouraging regular feedback and open communication is another crucial strategy for conflict prevention.

Understanding and effectively managing conflicts is critical for managers in modern workplaces' dynamic and often high-pressure environments.

By recognizing the different types of conflicts, employing constructive resolution techniques, mediating impartially, and taking proactive measures to prevent conflicts, you can create a more cohesive, collaborative, and high-performing team.

Active listening to both parties

Fostering a Culture of Continuous Improvement

Fostering a culture of continuous improvement is not merely a strategic advantage but a necessity (Deming, 1986).[1] The core principles that underpin this culture are a commitment to ongoing learning and development and an encouragement of experimentation and innovation. These principles are the bedrock upon which a dynamic, resilient, and forward-thinking organization is built. Commitment to ongoing learning involves creating an environment where knowledge acquisition is continuous and professional development is actively encouraged. This keeps the team abreast of the latest industry trends and technologies and enhances their skill sets, making them more adaptable and versatile. On the other hand, encouraging experimentation and innovation involves fostering a mindset that views failures and setbacks not as insurmountable obstacles but as opportunities for learning and growth. This mindset encourages team members to take calculated risks, think outside the box, and explore new ideas without fearing punitive consequences.

To implement these principles effectively, structured frameworks for continuous improvement can be introduced. One such framework is the Plan-Do-Check-Act (PDCA) cycle, a four-stage iterative problem-solving and process improvement approach. The PDCA cycle begins with the Plan phase, where the problem is identified, data is collected, and hypotheses are developed. The Do phase, which follows this one, involves putting a solution into practice on a small scale to gauge its efficacy. The check phase analyzes the implementation results to determine whether the solution has achieved the desired outcomes. Finally, the Act phase entails adopting the successful solution on a broader scale and making necessary adjustments. The PDCA cycle promotes a culture of continuous learning and improvement by systematically testing and refining solutions.

Fostering a growth mindset within the team is crucial for sustaining a culture of continuous improvement. This involves celebrating successes and viewing failures as valuable learning opportunities. By recognizing and rewarding achievements, managers can motivate team members to strive for excellence. Equally important is the ability to learn from failures. When setbacks occur, managers should encourage team members to analyze what went wrong instead of assigning blame, extract lessons, and apply these insights to future endeavors. Providing skill development and training opportunities is another key aspect of fostering a growth mindset. This can be achieved through workshops, seminars, online courses, and mentorship programs. By investing in their professional development, managers not only enhance the competencies of their team members but also signal that continuous learning is valued and supported.

In conclusion, fostering a culture of continuous improvement involves a commitment to learning, structured frameworks, and a growth mindset. These elements create a dynamic environment where teams can thrive and drive sustained success. The next chapter will delve into the nuances of stress management, exploring techniques to maintain well-being and productivity in high-pressure environments.

Downloadable Resources

To complement this chapter, the following resources are available for download at the end of Chapter 15:

a. Plan-Do-Check- Act. (PDCA) worksheet

Stress Management and Preventing Burnout

Stress Management and Preventing Burnout

Amid the fast-moving demands of today's work environment, consider the case of Laura, a project manager at a leading software development firm. Laura's team was in the final stages of delivering a groundbreaking product, but as deadlines loomed, she noticed a palpable shift in the team's dynamics. Productivity waned, morale dipped, and even her most resilient team members exhibited signs of weariness. Laura felt the mounting pressure, caught between senior management's expectations and her team's well-being. This scenario, a microcosm of broader organizational challenges, underscores the importance of understanding and managing workplace stress.

Identifying Stressors in the Workplace

Recognizing the typical sources of stress within a work environment is the first step in addressing and mitigating their impact. High workloads and tight deadlines are among the most pervasive stressors (Smith & Jones, 2020).[1] The relentless pursuit of targets, often coupled with the expectation of overtime, creates a pressure-cooker atmosphere that can erode mental and physical health. Employees inundated with tasks and constrained by time may feel overwhelmed, reducing productivity and engagement. Furthermore, the lack of control over work-related decisions exacerbates this stress. When employees feel they have limited control over their roles, their sense of autonomy fades, leading to frustration and helplessness. This can manifest in a disengaged workforce, where a rigid hierarchical structure stifles creativity and initiative.

Poor work-life balance contributes to workplace stress (Johnson, 2019).[2] Blurring boundaries between professional and personal life, especially in an era of remote work and constant connectivity, leaves employees with little respite. The expectation to be perpetually available, to respond to emails at all hours, and to sacrifice personal time for work commitments leads to chronic stress and burnout. This imbalance not only affects individual well-being but also impacts organizational productivity and morale. Employees who cannot recharge and disconnect from work are more likely to experience fatigue and decreased job satisfaction, leading to higher turnover rates.

Stress audits are an effective strategy for managers to identify team stressors systematically. Surveys and questionnaires can offer useful insights into the causes and levels of stress that employees experience. When designed thoughtfully, these tools can capture a wide range of stress indicators, from workload and job satisfaction to work-life balance and organizational support. One-on-one interviews and team meetings offer a more qualitative approach, allowing managers to delve deeper into individual experiences and perceptions. These conversations provide a platform for employees to voice their concerns and suggest potential solutions, fostering a culture of transparency and collaboration.

Recognizing the signs and symptoms of stress is crucial for timely intervention. Behavioral changes, such as irritability, withdrawal, and decreased motivation, are often the first indicators. Employees may become more prone to conflicts, exhibit reduced enthusiasm for their work, or isolate themselves from colleagues. Physical symptoms, including fatigue, headaches, and gastrointestinal issues, are common manifestations of stress. These symptoms, often overlooked, can significantly impair an employee's ability to perform and contribute effectively. Managers must observe and proactively address these signs, ensuring that employees receive support.

The impact of unaddressed stress is profound and far-reaching. Decreased productivity and job satisfaction are immediate consequences as stressed employees struggle to maintain their performance and engagement. Over time, this can lead to increased absenteeism and turnover rates, further straining organizational resources and disrupting team dynamics. The cumulative effect of chronic stress not only undermines individual well-being but also erodes the overall health and efficiency of the organization. Managers must recognize stress as a significant issue and implement strategies to mitigate its impact, fostering a supportive and resilient work environment.

Stress Audit Checklist

- Surveys and Questionnaires:

  - Frequency: Quarterly

  - Focus Areas: Workload, job satisfaction, work-life balance, organizational support

  - Sample Questions: "How often do you feel overwhelmed by your workload?" "Do you feel you have sufficient control over your work-related decisions?"

- One-on-One Interviews:

  - Frequency: Bi-monthly

  - Focus Areas: Individual experiences, perceptions, suggestions for improvement

  - Sample Questions: "What aspects of your job do you find most stressful?" "What changes would help you manage your stress better?"

- Team Meetings:

  - Frequency: Monthly

  - Focus Areas: Collective stressors, team dynamics, collaborative solutions

  - Sample Agenda: Review of survey results, open discussion on stressors, brainstorming session for solutions

By implementing regular stress audits and remaining vigilant to the signs and symptoms of stress, managers can create a proactive strategy that addresses the root causes of workplace stress, ultimately fostering a healthier, more productive work environment.

Mindfulness and Relaxation Techniques

Mindfulness, a practice with ancient roots, has become increasingly relevant in modern workplaces for its significant benefits in stress reduction and overall well-being. At its core, mindfulness involves developing a heightened awareness of the present moment, enabling individuals to respond to stressors with greater clarity and calmness. In the workplace, mindfulness practices have a wide-ranging positive impact. One of the most immediate benefits is improved focus and concentration. By training the mind to stay present, employees can enhance their attention span, minimize distractions, and boost productivity. Additionally, mindfulness supports emotional regulation, helping individuals manage their reactions to stress more effectively. This emotional resilience enhances personal well-being and contributes to a more harmonious and collaborative work environment.

Introducing mindfulness exercises for managers and teams can significantly lessen workplace stress. Simple techniques such as deep breathing and meditation can seamlessly integrate into the workday, providing immediate relief from stress and enhancing mental clarity. For instance, taking a few minutes to practice deep breathing can activate the body's relaxation response, reducing cortisol levels and promoting a sense of calm. Mindful walking, another accessible practice, involves walking slowly and deliberately, paying attention to each step and the sensations it brings. This exercise can be beneficial during breaks, allowing employees to recharge and return to tasks with renewed focus. Body scans, where individuals mentally scan their bodies from head to toe, noting areas of tension and consciously relaxing them, can also be a powerful tool for stress relief.

Physical activity and exercise are equally effective in managing stress. Encouraging team members to incorporate movement into their day can profoundly benefit physical and mental health. Walking meetings, for example, break the monotony of sitting and stimulate creative thinking and collaboration. Stretching breaks, whether individual or group activities, can alleviate physical tension and enhance overall well-being. These practices promote a healthier workplace and foster a culture of wellness and mutual support.

Incorporating mindfulness into daily routines requires planning and commitment. Scheduling short mindfulness breaks throughout the day can provide a much-needed respite from work demands. These breaks, even if just a few minutes long, can significantly reduce stress and improve focus. Utilizing mindfulness apps and resources can also be beneficial. Apps like Headspace and Calm offer guided meditations, breathing exercises, and mindfulness reminders, making it easier for employees to integrate these practices into their routines. Providing access to these resources and encouraging their use can create a supportive environment where mindfulness becomes a valued part of the organizational culture.

Case studies of successful mindfulness programs highlight the transformative potential of these practices. A leading tech company, for instance, implemented daily meditation sessions as part of their employee wellness program. The results were striking: employees reported reduced stress levels, improved focus, and greater well-being.

This example underscores the tangible benefits of mindfulness, demonstrating its efficacy in fostering a healthier, more productive workplace.

> "Almost everything will work again if you unplug it for a few minutes, including you."
> – Anne Lamott

Promoting Work-Life Balance

The significance of maintaining a balance between work and personal life cannot be overstated, as it plays a pivotal role in preventing burnout and enhancing overall well-being. When employees achieve a harmonious balance between their professional responsibilities and personal lives, they experience improved mental and physical health, leading to greater resilience against stress. This equilibrium fosters a sense of fulfillment and satisfaction, allowing individuals to engage fully in both spheres without feeling overwhelmed or depleted. Moreover, a well-balanced work-life dynamic contributes to heightened job satisfaction and performance, as employees who feel supported in their personal lives are more likely to bring their best selves to work, demonstrating increased motivation, creativity, and productivity.

Managers can implement several practical strategies to support their team's work-life balance. One effective approach is to encourage flexible work arrangements, such as remote work, flexible hours, or compressed workweeks. By allowing employees to manage their schedules, managers empower them to balance their work commitments with personal obligations, reducing stress and enhancing job satisfaction (Green, 2021).[3] Additionally, setting clear expectations regarding work hours and availability can help delineate boundaries, ensuring employees are not pressured to be constantly "on call." This clarity fosters a culture of respect for personal time, allowing team members to disconnect and recharge without guilt or anxiety.

Another strategy involves promoting a culture of time management and prioritization. Managers can lead by example, demonstrating the importance of setting realistic goals, delegating tasks appropriately, and avoiding unnecessary meetings. Encouraging employees to prioritize their workload and focus on high-impact tasks while delegating or deferring less critical activities can prevent the accumulation of stress and burnout. Training and resources on time management techniques, such as the Eisenhower Matrix or the Pomodoro Technique, can further equip team members to manage their time effectively, fostering a sense of control and reducing overwhelm.

Promoting regular breaks and downtime is also crucial for maintaining work-life balance. Managers should advocate for short, frequent breaks throughout the day, allowing employees to step away from their desks and engage in activities that promote relaxation and well-being. Whether it's a brief walk, a mindfulness exercise, or simply stretching, these breaks can significantly reduce stress and enhance focus and productivity. It is equally important to encourage employees to take their allotted vacation time and ensure that workloads are managed in their absence. By valuing and supporting time off, managers signal that personal well-being is prioritized, fostering a culture of balance and respect.

Maintain a balanced lifestyle.

Creating a supportive work environment that acknowledges and accommodates personal responsibilities can also enhance work-life balance. Managers should strive to understand their team members' unique needs and challenges, offering support and flexibility where possible. This might involve providing resources for childcare, eldercare, or other personal responsibilities or simply being understanding and accommodating during times of personal crisis. By demonstrating empathy and support, managers can build a culture of trust and loyalty where employees feel valued and respected as professionals and individuals.

Implementing wellness programs addressing physical, mental, and emotional health can promote work-life balance. These programs might include fitness classes, mental health resources, stress management workshops, and wellness challenges. Providing access to these resources and encouraging participation can help employees develop healthy habits, manage stress effectively, and maintain a balanced lifestyle. Additionally, fostering a culture of open communication and feedback allows employees to voice their needs and concerns, enabling managers to make informed decisions that support work-life balance.

Building Resilience and Coping Strategies

Understanding resilience is pivotal in the modern workplace, particularly regarding managing stress effectively. At its core, resilience refers to the ability to bounce back from setbacks and maintain a positive outlook even during challenging times. This quality is not innate but can be developed and enhanced through deliberate practice and self-awareness. Resilient individuals possess the mental fortitude to navigate adversities without succumbing to despair or defeat (Taylor, 2016). They view challenges as opportunities for growth rather than insurmountable obstacles. By cultivating resilience, you can better manage the inevitable stresses of professional life, maintaining your equilibrium and effectiveness even in the face of significant pressure.

Several techniques can bolster personal resilience, enabling you to withstand and recover from stress more effectively. Developing a solid support network is one such method. Surrounding yourself with colleagues, mentors, and friends who can offer advice, encouragement, and a listening ear can provide a vital buffer against stress. This network is a safety net, offering practical assistance and emotional support. Practicing self-care and healthy habits is another critical component. Regular exercise, a balanced diet, and sufficient sleep are foundational to physical and mental health.

Setting realistic goals and expectations is equally important. Breaking down large tasks into manageable steps and celebrating small achievements can help you maintain motivation and avoid feeling overwhelmed.

Coping strategies for stress management are essential tools for maintaining resilience. Practical problem-solving techniques can help you address the root causes of stress rather than merely alleviating its symptoms. When faced with a stressful situation, take a systematic approach to identify the problem, generate potential solutions, evaluate their feasibility, and implement the best course of action. This systematic approach can reduce helplessness and increase your sense of control. Time management skills are also crucial. Prioritizing tasks, setting clear deadlines, and avoiding procrastination can prevent the accumulation of stress and ensure you stay on top of your responsibilities. Engaging in hobbies and activities outside work provides respite from professional demands. Whether painting, gardening, playing a musical instrument, or participating in sports, these activities offer a creative and physical outlet for stress, promoting relaxation and mental clarity.

I remember when one of my team members, Laura, was balancing work with caring for her seriously ill parent. She didn't want to lose income by taking time off, but the stress of handling both was clearly affecting her. To support her, I encouraged resilience-building within the team and discussed openly how we could help. Without hesitation, others volunteered to temporarily take on some of her tasks, which allowed Laura to spend more time with her parent without feeling overwhelmed or financially strained. This experience not only helped Laura maintain stability but also strengthened our team, creating a supportive environment where everyone felt valued, both personally and professionally.

In conclusion, building resilience and employing effective coping strategies are vital in managing workplace stress and maintaining overall well-being. Developing a solid support network, practicing self-care, setting realistic goals, and utilizing practical coping mechanisms can enhance resilience and help you navigate professional challenges with confidence and poise.

The next chapter will explore the transition from manager to leader, delving into the skills and mindsets necessary to inspire and motivate your team effectively. This transition is crucial in fostering a culture of trust, collaboration, and innovation, ultimately driving organizational success.

Transitioning from Manager to Leader

In the peaceful moments before dawn, Allison, a dedicated manager at a rapidly expanding financial firm, stood on her balcony, contemplating the transition from managing tasks to inspiring her team. She realized that her role demanded more than meticulous planning and efficient task execution; it required a profound shift in mindset—a journey from manager to leader. This transformation was about evolving into a figure who could galvanize, influence, and steer her team toward a shared vision with unwavering commitment and integrity.

Developing a Leadership Mindset

Understanding the leadership mindset is crucial in distinguishing between managing and leading. A managerial mindset is often anchored in executing predefined tasks, ensuring that processes run smoothly and objectives are met within the constraints of time and resources. Managers excel in planning, organizing, and controlling, focusing on the "how" and "when" of task completion. In contrast, a leadership mindset transcends these operational confines, emphasizing vision and direction over task management. Leaders ask "what" and "why," seeking to understand the broader purpose behind actions and decisions. They are visionaries who craft pathways for organizational growth, inspiring their teams to align with a collective mission.

The essence of leadership lies in influence rather than authority. While managers may rely on hierarchical power to achieve compliance, leaders cultivate influence by building trust and demonstrating authenticity. This influence is not wielded through coercion but earned through consistent, ethical behavior and genuine concern for team members' development. Leaders inspire their teams to exceed expectations, fostering an environment where individuals are motivated by a shared purpose rather than mere obligation.

Cultivating self-awareness and personal growth is fundamental to adopting a leadership mindset. Continuous self-improvement and reflection enable leaders to understand their strengths and areas for development. Regular self-assessments, such as the DISC or Myers-Briggs Type Indicator (MBTI), provide valuable insights into one's leadership style and interpersonal dynamics (Robbins, 2020).[1] Feedback loops, involving input from peers and subordinates, offer a 360-degree view of performance, highlighting blind spots and areas for refinement. Setting personal development goals, informed by these assessments, ensures that growth is deliberate and aligned with the demands of leadership.

Embracing change and innovation is a key characteristic of effective leadership. Leaders need to be receptive to new ideas and adaptable to evolving circumstances. This means actively promoting innovation and guiding change initiatives within the organization. By encouraging a culture of creativity and continuous improvement, leaders help build an environment where experimentation is welcomed, and setbacks are viewed as learning opportunities. This proactive approach keeps the organization flexible and competitive in a rapidly changing environment.

Leaders who embody these principles—visionary thinking, influence over authority, continuous self-improvement, adaptability to change, and emotional intelligence—set the stage for a transformative leadership experience. As you embark on this journey, remember that the transition from manager to leader is not a destination but an ongoing process of growth and evolution.

Inspiring and Motivating Your Team

Crafting a compelling vision is fundamental to inspiring and motivating your team. A vision statement is a beacon, guiding and aligning the team's collective efforts toward a shared objective. It is not merely a statement of intent but a vivid portrayal of a desired future that resonates deeply with team members. Understanding your team's core values and aspirations involves crafting a vision that captures the imagination. This vision should be ambitious yet attainable, encouraging everyone to strive for excellence. The vision must be communicated effectively and consistently, woven into daily operations and decision-making processes. By reiterating the vision through meetings, communications, and even visual reminders like posters, you ensure that it remains at the forefront of everyone's mind, fostering a sense of purpose and direction.

Setting high but achievable expectations is a delicate balance that can significantly impact team motivation. Stretch goals encourage team members to move beyond their comfort zones, promoting growth and innovation. These goals should be challenging enough to inspire effort and creativity but realistic enough to be attainable with dedicated effort. Providing the necessary resources and guidance is crucial in this context. As a leader, you must equip your team with the tools, training, and support they need to meet these heightened expectations. This may involve facilitating access to advanced software, offering professional development opportunities, or providing clear and constructive feedback. By setting the bar high and backing it up with tangible support, you empower your team to achieve remarkable results, fostering a culture of continuous improvement and resilience.

Recognizing and rewarding achievements plays a pivotal role in maintaining team motivation. Formal recognition programs, such as employee of the month awards or performance-based bonuses, provide structured avenues for acknowledging exceptional contributions. These programs should be transparent and based on clearly defined criteria to ensure fairness and credibility. However, recognition need not always be formal. Spontaneous, informal praise can be equally impactful. A simple gesture like a heartfelt thank-you note, a shout-out in a team meeting, or an impromptu celebratory lunch can significantly make team members feel valued and appreciated. Even just a simple 'thanks for your hard work today, guys, as they head out the door is a nice touch. Recognition validates the effort and dedication of team members, reinforcing positive behaviors and boosting morale. It creates a virtuous cycle where motivated employees are more likely to go above and beyond, contributing to a high-performance culture.

A positive and inclusive culture is essential in creating an environment where team members feel valued and motivated. Encouraging diversity and inclusion involves more than just adhering to policies; it requires a genuine commitment to embracing and celebrating differences. This can be achieved by promoting diverse hiring practices, providing cultural competency training, and creating platforms for underrepresented voices to be heard. An inclusive culture enriches the team with various perspectives and ideas, driving innovation and collaboration. Promoting teamwork and collaboration further strengthens this culture. Facilitating team-building activities, encouraging cross-functional projects, and fostering open communication channels create a sense of camaraderie and mutual respect. When team members feel part of a supportive and cohesive unit, they are more likely to be engaged and motivated, contributing to the organization's overall success.

Leading by Example

Modeling desired behaviors is a cornerstone of effective leadership, providing a tangible benchmark for team members to emulate. When leaders demonstrate commitment and dedication to their work, they set a powerful precedent that resonates throughout the organization. This level of engagement is not merely about clocking in hours but about showing a genuine investment in the team's success and the organization's objectives. Practicing transparency and honesty further solidifies this example, fostering an environment where trust and open communication flourish. When leaders are forthright about their decisions, including the rationale and potential impacts, they demystify the leadership process, encouraging a culture where team members feel valued and included in the organizational discourse.

Inspire your team

Maintaining high ethical standards profoundly influences team behavior and organizational culture. Leaders who uphold integrity in all decisions and actions create a moral compass that guides the team. This ethical framework is crucial, especially in challenging situations where the temptation to compromise values for short-term gains is strong. Addressing unethical behavior promptly and fairly reinforces this commitment to integrity, signaling to the team that ethical lapses will not be tolerated. Such decisive action rectifies the immediate issue and deters future transgressions, fostering a culture of accountability and ethical rigor. By consistently demonstrating ethical behavior, leaders inspire their teams to adopt similar standards, thereby enhancing the overall ethical climate of the organization.

A leader's work ethic sets the tone for the entire team, establishing a benchmark for performance and dedication. Consistently meeting and exceeding performance expectations exemplifies the high standards that leaders expect from their team members. This consistency is not about relentless perfectionism but about demonstrating a robust commitment to excellence and continuous improvement. Balancing hard work with strategic thinking is equally important. Leaders must be diligent and visionary, ensuring their efforts align with long-term goals and strategic objectives. This balance ensures the team's hard work translates into meaningful progress and sustainable success. When leaders embody a strong work ethic, it cultivates a culture of diligence and strategic foresight, motivating team members to elevate their standards and contributions.

Encouraging continuous learning and development is another critical aspect of leading by example. Leaders who prioritize their growth inspire their teams to do the same. Participating in professional development opportunities, such as attending workshops, earning certifications, or pursuing advanced degrees, signals to the team that learning is a lifelong pursuit. Sharing knowledge and insights gained from these experiences further amplifies this message, creating a culture of collective growth and intellectual curiosity. When leaders actively engage in learning and development, they demonstrate that pursuing knowledge is integral to professional success and organizational advancement. This commitment to growth enhances the leader's capabilities and elevates the team's overall skill set and adaptability.

Moreover, fostering an environment where continuous learning is valued encourages team members to seek opportunities for their development. This could involve supporting attendance at industry conferences, facilitating access to online courses, or providing resources for skill enhancement. By investing in their team's growth, leaders cultivate a culture where innovation and improvement are encouraged and expected. This proactive approach to development ensures that the team remains competitive, resilient, and prepared to meet the industry's evolving demands. When leaders lead by example in this way, they create a dynamic and progressive work environment where both individuals and the organization can thrive.

Mentoring and Developing Future Leaders

Identifying potential leaders within your team is a nuanced process that requires an astute understanding of the qualities that signify leadership potential (Goleman, 1998).[2] These traits often manifest in individuals who exhibit consistent initiative, taking proactive steps to address challenges and seize opportunities without waiting for directives. Such individuals demonstrate a profound sense of responsibility, owning their tasks and outcomes and being willing to go above and beyond their defined roles. Their communication skills are another critical indicator; influential leaders are adept at conveying ideas, listening actively, and fostering open dialogue within the team. Observing how team members handle challenges is equally important. Those who approach obstacles with a problem-solving mindset, exhibit resilience under pressure and maintain a positive attitude are likely candidates for leadership roles. While not exhaustive, these traits provide a robust framework for recognizing potential leaders.

Once identified, providing mentorship and guidance to these emerging leaders is paramount. Effective mentorship involves more than occasional advice; it requires regular, structured interactions that facilitate growth and development. One-on-one coaching sessions offer a personalized approach to address individual strengths and areas for improvement, providing a safe space for mentees to discuss challenges, seek advice, and reflect on their progress. Formal mentorship programs can institutionalize this process, pairing experienced leaders with potential ones and creating a structured pathway for skill transfer and professional growth. Such programs should encourage regular feedback, goal setting, and progress tracking, ensuring that mentorship is purposeful and impactful.

Creating development opportunities is crucial in nurturing future leaders. Assigning challenging projects and stretch assignments allows potential leaders to step outside their comfort zones and test their abilities in real-world scenarios. These assignments should be strategically chosen to align with the individual's career aspirations and developmental needs, providing a balanced mix of challenge and support. Encouraging participation in leadership training programs further enhances their growth. These programs can range from formal courses and workshops to experiential learning opportunities such as leading cross-functional teams or participating in strategic planning sessions. Exposing future leaders to diverse experiences and perspectives equips them with the skills and confidence to navigate complex leadership challenges.

Building a succession plan ensures leadership continuity within the organization, safeguarding against the disruptions that can occur with sudden leadership changes (Rothwell, 2010).[3] This process begins with identifying key roles critical to the organization's success and pinpointing potential successors for these positions. A structured succession plan outlines the competencies required for each role, the developmental pathways for potential successors, and the timelines for their readiness. Regularly reviewing and updating this plan is essential to ensure its relevance and effectiveness. This involves assessing the progress of potential successors, adjusting development plans as needed, and aligning the succession strategy with the organization's evolving goals and challenges.

By fostering an environment where potential leaders are identified, mentored, and provided with growth opportunities and ensuring a robust succession plan is in place, you create a pipeline of capable leaders ready to drive the organization forward. This holistic approach not only strengthens leadership within the team but also contributes to the long-term resilience and success of the organization.

As you continue cultivating these future leaders, you contribute to a legacy of excellence and innovation, setting the stage for sustained organizational growth and success.

> "The function of leadership is to produce more leaders, not more followers."
> – Ralph Nader

Downloadable Resources

To give you a bit of extra help with what we've covered in this chapter, you'll find the following resources at the end of Chapter 15:

a. What does 100% look like? Entrepreneur Circle.

b. DISC assessment https://www.tonyrobbins.com/disc four primary personality types – dominance, influence, steadiness, and conscientiousness. Link to FREE online test.

Transitioning from Peer to Manager

Navigating the shift from peer to manager presents unique challenges in a large corporation or a small business. Consider Jessica, recently promoted to a managerial position in the same department where she once worked alongside her peers. The transition from peer to manager is fraught with complexities, necessitating a delicate balance between maintaining camaraderie and asserting authority. Jessica's journey encapsulates the quintessential challenges many newly minted managers face, who must redefine relationships without losing the trust and respect that constitutes the foundation of effective leadership.

Establishing Authority and Building Trust

Establishing authority without coming across as overly authoritative is essential for new managers. Striking the right balance between approachability and assertiveness helps you gain your team's respect and trust while avoiding the risk of seeming too domineering. One of the most effective ways to achieve this is by role-modeling the behaviors you want to see in your team, such as punctuality, dedication, and ethical conduct. Leading by example sets a powerful standard and inspires your team to follow suit.

Consistency in decision-making is another critical factor. When your decisions are fair, thoughtful, and consistent, it creates a sense of stability and predictability that fosters trust within your team. Equally important is showing empathy while maintaining professionalism. By understanding your team members' challenges, goals, and concerns without compromising your role as a leader, you build an environment of mutual respect and collaboration that supports individual and collective success.

Certain actions are highly effective in building trust within a team. Start by personalizing your leadership approach through one-on-one meetings with team members. These conversations provide an opportunity to understand their goals, concerns, and motivations while fostering open dialogue. Proactively addressing issues during these meetings shows genuine interest in their well-being and builds rapport.

Transparent communication is another essential element of trust. Keeping your team informed about the reasoning behind decisions, the impact of changes, and the team's strategic direction creates an environment of openness and reliability. Additionally, recognizing contributions and giving credit where it's due is crucial. Publicly acknowledging the efforts and achievements of your team members not only boosts morale but also reinforces a culture of appreciation and respect, strengthening the bonds within the team.

Leading by example is perhaps the most potent tool when establishing authority. Demonstrating punctuality and commitment to your work sets a standard for your team. You must exhibit the same dedication if you expect your team to adhere to deadlines and maintain high professionalism. Upholding company values and ethical standards in all your actions underscores your integrity and reinforces the importance of these principles within the team. Participating in team activities and showing solidarity with your team members further bridges the gap between manager and team. Engaging in collaborative projects, attending team-building events, and being present in day-to-day activities demonstrates your investment in the team's success.

I remember the challenges of transitioning from peer to manager in my mid-twenties, especially with older colleagues. I started with an introductory email outlining my role, vision, and anticipated changes to ease the shift, ensuring the message resonated with each team member. I then held individual meetings to address any potential awkwardness, inviting them to share their thoughts and goals. This approach helped lay a foundation of trust and inclusion.

To keep communication transparent, I scheduled regular team meetings for updates and maintained a mix of emails, team chats, and face-to-face conversations to ensure clarity. I also made it a point to recognize the team's achievements and set an example through commitment and integrity. Engaging in team activities and fostering a shared purpose helped the team quickly adjust, leading to a more unified and cohesive environment.

To help you apply these principles, consider engaging in scenario-based exercises where you practice giving constructive feedback. Reflect on situations where you might need to address performance issues with a former peer. Role-play these scenarios, focusing on maintaining a balance between empathy and professionalism. Reflective questions about your leadership style and improvement areas can also be valuable. For instance, ask yourself: How do I handle difficult conversations? Do I maintain consistency in my decisions? How can I better demonstrate empathy while upholding professional standards? You can establish authority and build lasting trust with your team in these ways.

Setting Clear Expectations with Former Peers

As you transition from peer to manager, setting clear expectations becomes a linchpin for maintaining productivity and avoiding confusion. Articulating your expectations precisely ensures that everyone on the team understands their roles, responsibilities, and the standards they hold. Specific goals and objectives provide a roadmap for the team, aligning individual efforts with broader organizational aims. Clear articulation of these goals mitigates ambiguity, ensuring each team member knows precisely what is expected. Outlining roles and responsibilities is equally vital, as it delineates the scope of each person's duties, preventing overlaps and fostering accountability. Setting performance standards and metrics offers a tangible yardstick against which progress can be measured, facilitating regular assessments and adjustments.

Conducting expectation-setting meetings is a strategic process that requires meticulous preparation and execution. You can begin by preparing a detailed agenda that outlines the key points to be discussed. This agenda should include the specific goals, roles, responsibilities, and performance metrics to be addressed, ensuring that the meeting remains focused and productive. Encouraging open dialogue and feedback during these meetings is crucial. Foster an environment where team members feel comfortable voicing their thoughts, concerns, and suggestions. This enhances buy-in and provides valuable insights to refine the expectations. Documenting and distributing the agreed-upon goals to the team ensures that everyone has a clear reference point, reducing the likelihood of misunderstandings and misaligned efforts.

Consistency in enforcing expectations is paramount for maintaining trust and authority. Regularly reviewing and tracking progress against the established goals and metrics allows you to identify areas where the team excels, and improvements are needed. Address deviations from expectations quickly and constructively, providing support and resources to help team members get back on track. This consistent approach reinforces the importance of the established goals and standards, fostering a culture of accountability and continuous improvement.

Sample Expectation-Setting Meeting Agenda

1. Introduction

    ○ Welcome, and purpose of the meeting.

2. Review of Team Goals

    ○ Goals-Specific objectives for the upcoming period.

3. Roles and Responsibilities

    ○ Detailed outline of each team member's duties.

4. Performance Standards and Metrics

    ○ Criteria for measuring success.

5. Open Dialogue and Feedback

    ○ Encouraging team members to share their thoughts and concerns.

6. Documentation and Distribution

    ○ Summary of agreed-upon goals and next steps.

Adhering to these structured processes and principles can help you effectively set clear expectations with your former peers, ensuring a smooth transition to your new role and a team that remains aligned and productive.

Communicating Your New Role Effectively

The transition from peer to manager involves more than just a title change; it requires a fundamental shift in how you communicate your new role to the team. Effective communication is the linchpin in managing team dynamics and reducing resistance. Clarity about the scope of your new responsibilities is paramount. By elucidating the boundaries of your new role and articulating the responsibilities that come with it, you set the stage for a smoother transition. Addressing potential concerns and questions from the team is equally vital. This proactive approach mitigates uncertainties and fosters an environment of openness and trust. Highlighting how your new role benefits both the team and the organization provides a broader context, reinforcing the positive aspects of this transition. Active listening and feedback are critical components of effective communication during this transition.

Navigating Friendship and Professional Boundaries

Managing former peers presents a labyrinth of complexities that requires careful navigation to maintain professional boundaries while preserving friendships. The challenge lies in redefining relationships without eroding the camaraderie that once existed. Setting clear boundaries between work and personal life is imperative. This means delineating the lines of authority at work while ensuring personal interactions remain unaffected. Communicating your need for professionalism at work is crucial; let your friends-turned-colleagues know that while you value friendship, professional responsibilities require a different dynamic during work hours. Balancing social interactions with professional responsibilities is equally important. Engage in social activities, but be mindful of the context and ensure that professional duties are not compromised.

Specific actions can be highly effective in maintaining professional relationships. Avoiding favoritism and treating all team members equally is paramount. This ensures no one feels alienated or undervalued, preserving team cohesion and morale. Transparency about the changes in the relationship helps in setting clear expectations. For instance, acknowledging that your role has changed and explaining how it impacts interactions can mitigate misunderstandings. Seeking support from other managers or mentors can provide additional insights and strategies. Their experience can offer valuable perspectives on effectively navigating the dual roles of friend and manager.

There are numerous potential pitfalls in managing former peers, but they can be avoided with foresight and strategic actions. Avoiding gossip and maintaining confidentiality is critical. Engaging in gossip can undermine your credibility and erode trust. Recognizing and addressing conflicts of interest is also essential. If personal relationships might influence professional decisions, handling them transparently and somewhat is vital. Managing social media interactions appropriately is another aspect to consider. While social media can be a platform for maintaining personal connections, it is crucial to ensure that professional boundaries are respected. Avoid sharing work-related issues and maintain a professional demeanor in all interactions.

Set clear boundaries, maintaining professional relationships,

Reflective Exercise: Setting Boundaries in Professional Relationships

Reflect on a recent situation where you had to navigate the dual roles of friend and manager. Consider the following prompts:

- How did you handle the transition from peer to manager?

- What strategies did you use to set clear boundaries?

- How did you communicate your need for professionalism at work?

- What challenges did you face, and how did you address them?

Use this reflection to identify areas for improvement in your approach to managing professional relationships. Consider seeking feedback from your team and mentors to gain additional insights and refine your strategies.

In summary, transitioning from peer to manager involves navigating complex relationships and responsibilities. You can effectively manage this transition by setting clear boundaries, maintaining professional relationships, avoiding potential pitfalls, and reflecting on your experiences. This approach preserves friendships, establishes your authority, and fosters a cohesive and productive team environment. As you refine your management skills, remember that this transition is a continuous process of learning and adaptation, essential for your growth as a leader.

Navigating Organizational Politics

Power dynamics weave a complex web that shapes the daily workflow in small and large organizations. Picture a newly appointed project manager, David, stepping into a high-visibility, politically charged project. His role extends beyond simply meeting project milestones; he must also navigate the intricate power relationships underpinning the organizational structure. Understanding these dynamics is critical, as they significantly influence decision-making, team cohesion, and overall organizational effectiveness.

Understanding Power Dynamics

Power dynamics refer to how authority is distributed and exercised, affecting interactions and outcomes at every level. Power can take a formal shape, stemming from an individual's position within the hierarchy, or an informal one, derived from personal influence and relationships. Recognizing and understanding formal and informal power structures is essential for successfully navigating the complexities of the corporate environment.

While formal power structures in larger organizations are often explicit and well-documented, with clear lines of authority and responsibility outlined in organizational charts, smaller businesses tend to be more fluid. In a small business, titles may hold less weight, and decision-making is often more collaborative or centralized within a few key individuals. In either case, understanding the power dynamics—whether formal or informal—is crucial for navigating how decisions are made and resources are allocated.

In contrast, informal power structures are subtler and less visible yet wield considerable influence. These structures are based on relationships, networks, and the social capital individuals accumulate within the organization. Key decision-makers and influencers within informal power structures may not hold prominent titles, but their ability to shape opinions, sway decisions, and mobilize support makes them pivotal players. Recognizing these informal influencers requires keen observation, active listening, and understanding the organization's social dynamics.

Different forms of power coexist within an organization, uniquely shaping interactions and outcomes. Positional power comes from an individual's role or title and is often linked to formal authority. For instance, a CFO wields positional power through their ability to make financial decisions that affect the entire organization. In contrast, personal power stems from relationships and expertise. Individuals with personal power may not hold formal titles, but their deep knowledge, experience, and ability to build trust and rapport give them considerable influence.

Reward and coercive power are also standard in organizational settings. Reward power influences behavior by offering incentives such as promotions, bonuses, or recognition. Conversely, coercive power relies on the threat of punishment or negative consequences to enforce compliance. While both forms of power can motivate and guide teams effectively, they must be used carefully to avoid creating resentment or fear.

Power dynamics profoundly impact team performance, influencing everything from communication patterns to decision-making processes. Power imbalances can lead to conflicts or misunderstandings, as individuals with less power may feel marginalized or undervalued. For instance, a team member who perceives their ideas as consistently ignored by a dominant colleague may become disengaged, diminishing overall team cohesion and productivity.

Conversely, the positive use of power can motivate and guide teams towards achieving collective goals. Leaders who leverage their power to empower others, provide clear direction, and foster an inclusive environment can enhance team performance. For example, a project manager who uses their positional power to allocate resources effectively and their power to build strong relationships can drive successful project outcomes.

Early in my career, I managed a challenging project where I had to balance the vision of a senior manager, Karen, with the practical needs of our operations and marketing teams. Karen's influence was substantial, but the challenges were real and couldn't be overlooked. To address this, I set up one-on-one discussions with her and key team members to create alignment.

Respecting Karen's authority and validating her goals helped me secure needed resources, but my relationships within the team made a real difference. When the marketing department hesitated due to resource constraints, I reached out to Tom, a key influencer in operations. His support was crucial in rallying both departments to move forward collaboratively.

Navigating these dynamics taught me that effective leadership in a politically charged setting requires strategic thinking and a strong network of relationships. It's about balancing interests and keeping team morale steady despite competing demands.

Reflection Exercise: Analyzing Your Organizational Power Dynamics

Spend some time reflecting on the power dynamics within your organization. Identify both formal and informal power structures, noting key decision-makers and influencers. Consider how these dynamics impact your team's interactions and outcomes. Reflect on your power sources and how you can leverage them to navigate organizational politics effectively.

Understanding and navigating power dynamics is critical for any manager or leader. By recognizing formal and informal power structures, identifying different types of power, and analyzing their impact on team performance, you can effectively maneuver through the complex web of organizational politics, fostering a more cohesive and productive work environment.

Building Alliances and Networks

Alliances and networks function as the connective threads that tie disparate elements together, enhancing your influence and support within the company. Forming partnerships is not merely a strategic advantage but a necessity for navigating the complex landscape of organizational politics. Alliances amplify your voice, enabling you to garner the support needed to advance initiatives and secure resources. They facilitate the flow of information, ensuring you are well-informed and can make decisions based on a comprehensive understanding of the organizational climate. Additionally, alliances foster resource sharing, allowing you to leverage the expertise, knowledge, and capabilities of others to achieve your goals more effectively. This interconnectedness is crucial in environments where collaboration and collective effort are the linchpins of success.

Building solid networks requires deliberate effort and strategic planning. One effective method is identifying and connecting with key stakeholders who hold influence and can provide valuable support. This involves mapping the organizational landscape to pinpoint individuals whose roles, responsibilities, and interests align with your objectives. Engaging with these stakeholders through formal and informal interactions helps establish rapport and trust. Participating in cross-functional teams and committees is another powerful strategy. These platforms offer opportunities to collaborate with colleagues from various departments, broadening your perspective and fostering a culture of cooperation. Cross-functional teams, in particular, integrate diverse skill sets and viewpoints, enhancing problem-solving and innovation. By actively contributing to these teams, you demonstrate your commitment to the organization's broader goals, making you a valuable ally.

Leveraging both internal and external networks is essential for achieving your objectives. Internally, collaborating with colleagues from different departments can break down silos and foster a more integrated approach to problem-solving (Cross, Ernst, & Pasmore, 2013).[1] For example, working closely with the finance department can provide insights into budget constraints and opportunities, enabling you to make more informed decisions. Externally, engaging with industry associations and professional groups expands your horizons and connects you with thought leaders and experts in your field. These external networks are invaluable for gaining new perspectives, staying updated on industry trends, and accessing resources that may not be available within your organization. By participating in conferences, webinars, and professional forums, you position yourself as a proactive and informed leader, enhancing your credibility and influence.

Reflection Exercise: Analyzing Your Networking Strategies

Reflect on your current networking strategies. Identify key organizational stakeholders and consider how you can strengthen these relationships. Assess your involvement in cross-functional teams and external industry groups. Develop a plan to enhance your professional network, focusing on internal and external connections. Consider setting specific goals, such as attending industry conferences or joining professional associations, to expand your reach and influence. Evaluate the effectiveness of your current strategies and make adjustments as needed to ensure you are leveraging your network to its fullest potential.

By building strong alliances and networks, you enhance your ability to navigate the complexities of organizational politics, secure support for your initiatives, and achieve your professional goals. These connections are beneficial and integral to your success in a dynamic and interconnected organizational environment.

Advocating for Your Team

Effective leadership necessitates a robust commitment to advocating for your team, ensuring they receive the recognition and resources essential for success. Advocacy is not merely about championing your team's immediate needs; it is about securing the necessary resources and support to enable them to thrive. This involves identifying resource gaps, negotiating with upper management for additional budget allocations, and ensuring that your team has access to the tools and training necessary to excel. Enhancing team visibility and credibility within the organization is equally crucial. By highlighting your team's achievements, you boost their morale and position them as invaluable contributors to the organization's goals. This visibility can lead to greater opportunities for your team members, fostering career growth and professional development.

Articulating team achievements and needs with clarity and precision is fundamental to effective advocacy. This involves presenting your team's accomplishments in a manner that aligns with the broader organizational objectives, ensuring that their contributions are recognized and valued. Building a compelling case often requires the use of data and testimonials. Quantitative metrics such as performance indicators, project completion rates, and efficiency improvements provide concrete evidence of your team's impact. Testimonials from satisfied clients or internal stakeholders add a qualitative dimension, offering personal insights into the value your team brings. Combining data with compelling narratives creates a persuasive argument that underscores the importance of supporting your team.

Balancing advocacy for your team with the organization's overall goals is delicate. It involves aligning your team's objectives with the company's strategic priorities, making it easier to secure support while demonstrating your team's critical role in the organization's success. Collaborating with other departments can further strengthen this alignment by creating mutual benefits. For example, partnering with the marketing department to highlight your team's contributions to a successful campaign can showcase interdepartmental synergy and its positive impact on the organization. Such collaboration can lead to shared resources, joint initiatives, and a more cohesive organizational culture, enhancing your team's position within the company.

> "In the end, people are not persuaded by what we say, but by what they understand."
> – John C. Maxwell

I remember when I needed additional resources for my department, which was stretched thin under a growing workload. To make a solid case, I gathered data on our recent achievements, like productivity gains, cost savings, and client feedback, showing how our work aligned with the company's broader goals.

I also contacted other department heads, including Anna in Sales and Mark in Marketing, to gather their support. I demonstrated our team's broader impact by highlighting how our efforts helped them close deals faster or run more effective campaigns. I even secured brief testimonials from senior executives directly benefiting from our work.

Presenting this mix of data, testimonials, and strategic alliances strengthened my case, and we ultimately received the resources we needed. This experience reinforced the power of aligning team goals with company priorities and building strong internal networks.

Advocating for your team is an ongoing process that requires a strategic approach, clear communication, and a profound understanding of your team's needs and the organization's goals. By effectively articulating achievements, building compelling cases with data and testimonials, and aligning team objectives with broader organizational priorities, you can ensure your team receives the support and recognition they deserve, fostering a culture of success and continuous improvement.

Managing Up: Influencing Senior Leaders

Building robust relationships with senior leaders and aligning your team's efforts with the broader objectives set forth by these decision-makers is essential. Managing up is about currying favor and fostering a symbiotic relationship where mutual goals are understood and pursued collaboratively. It is crucial to career advancement and team success, as it positions you and your team as indispensable assets within the organization. Building solid relationships with senior leaders necessitates an in-depth understanding of their priorities, communication styles, and expectations. This foundational knowledge allows you to tailor your interactions to resonate with them, fostering trust and credibility.

I remember presenting a project proposal to senior leaders and quickly realizing that understanding their priorities was key. Knowing they were short on time, I prepared a concise executive summary focusing on the project's benefits, potential challenges, and proposed solutions. This streamlined approach helped capture their attention without overloading them with details.

I also considered their communication preferences; some leaders preferred high-level overviews, while others appreciated brief insights on budget and outcomes. By adapting my presentation style to these preferences, I was able to keep them engaged and address their concerns efficiently.

Ultimately, this approach helped secure their support and reinforced my credibility as someone who could effectively deliver information. This experience showed me that genuinely influencing senior leaders means aligning your message with their priorities and preferences.

Balancing assertiveness with respect is critical to managing up. While it is essential to communicate your team's needs and achievements assertively, it is equally vital to do so with professionalism and respect for leadership decisions. Providing constructive feedback to senior leaders requires a delicate touch. It involves framing your insights in a way that highlights potential areas for improvement without undermining their authority. For example, if you notice inefficiencies in a new process implemented by senior management, presenting your observations alongside potential solutions can demonstrate your commitment to organizational success while respecting their leadership role. This approach fosters a culture of continuous improvement and positions you as a proactive and thoughtful contributor.

Managing up is an indispensable skill in the repertoire of effective leaders. By building solid relationships with senior leaders, understanding their priorities, communicating assertively yet respectfully, and aligning your team's efforts with organizational goals, you can navigate the complex dynamics of your workplace with confidence and foresight. This strategic approach enhances your team's success and propels your career forward, positioning you as a trusted and influential leader.

As we transition to the next chapter, we will explore the principles of effective time management. This critical skill complements your ability to navigate organizational politics and lead your team to success.

Effective Time Management

Time Management

In the early hours of a brisk autumn morning, Paul, a senior project manager at an innovative tech firm, grappled with an overwhelming array of tasks. His desk was a mosaic of sticky notes, each a reminder of an impending deadline or an urgent matter that demanded her immediate attention. Despite his meticulous planning, the sheer number of responsibilities threatened to derail his productivity. At this moment of chaos, Paul recalled a time-tested strategy he had once learned during a leadership seminar—the Eisenhower Matrix. This simple yet profound tool promised to bring order to his disarray and empower him to prioritize with precision.

Prioritizing Tasks with the Eisenhower Matrix

The Eisenhower Matrix, named after the 34th President of the United States, Dwight D. Eisenhower, is a task management tool that categorizes tasks based on urgency and importance (Eisenhower, 1954).[1] This matrix divides tasks into four quadrants, each representing a different priority level. The first quadrant, "Urgent and Important," encompasses tasks that require immediate attention and have significant consequences if not completed promptly. These crises, pressing problems, and deadline-driven projects demand your immediate focus. For instance, finalizing a project proposal due by the end of the day or addressing a critical client issue falls into this quadrant.

The second quadrant, "Important but Not Urgent," comprises tasks that are crucial for long-term success but do not require immediate action. These tasks often involve strategic planning, personal development, and relationship-building activities that, while not pressing, are essential for future growth. Examples include scheduling a professional development course, planning a quarterly strategy session, or investing time in networking events. These tasks should be scheduled into your calendar to ensure they receive the attention they deserve.

The third quadrant, "Urgent but Not Important," includes tasks that demand immediate attention but do not significantly contribute to your long-term goals. These tasks are often interruptions that can be delegated to others, allowing you to focus on more critical activities. Examples might be responding to routine emails, attending low-priority meetings, or handling minor administrative tasks. Delegating these tasks effectively frees up your time for more impactful work.

The fourth quadrant, "Neither Urgent nor Important," consists of tasks that offer little value and can often be eliminated. These are the time-wasters that clutter your schedule and detract from your productivity. Examples include unnecessary social media browsing, attending unproductive meetings, or engaging in trivial activities that do not align with your goals. By identifying and eliminating these tasks, you can streamline your workload and focus on what truly matters.

To utilize the Eisenhower Matrix effectively, list your current tasks and responsibilities. This comprehensive inventory serves as the foundation for categorizing and prioritizing your workload. Once you have your list, assess each task's urgency and importance. Consider the potential consequences of not completing the task promptly and its impact on your long-term objectives. This evaluation allows you to place each task into its appropriate quadrant.

For instance, imagine you have a list that includes finalizing a project report due tomorrow, planning a team-building event, responding to a non-urgent client email, and reviewing a new software tool. The project report would fall into the "Urgent and Important" quadrant, requiring immediate attention. Planning the team-building event, crucial for fostering team cohesion but not time-sensitive, would be categorized as "Important but Not Urgent." Responding to the non-urgent client email could be delegated to a team member, placing it in the "Urgent but Not Important" quadrant. Finally, reviewing the new software tool, which is neither urgent nor critical to your current goals, would be classified as "Neither Urgent nor Important."

The benefits of using the Eisenhower Matrix are extensive. By focusing on urgent and important tasks, you can reduce stress and ensure critical deadlines are met. Addressing important but not urgent tasks helps you avoid procrastination and make steady progress toward long-term goals. Delegating urgent but unimportant tasks optimizes your workflow, freeing you from less impactful responsibilities. Finally, eliminating tasks that are neither urgent nor important saves time and mental energy, allowing you to concentrate on what truly matters.

The practical application of the Eisenhower Matrix can be illustrated through scenarios and exercises. Consider Rachel, who, after categorizing her tasks, scheduled her important but not urgent tasks, such as planning the quarterly strategy session, into her calendar. She delegated routine email responses to her assistant, freeing time to focus on the project proposal. She invested additional hours in strategic planning by eliminating unnecessary social media browsing. This structured approach enabled Rachel to navigate her responsibilities with clarity and efficiency, ultimately enhancing her productivity and reducing stress.

Exercise: Using the Eisenhower Matrix

1. List Your Tasks: Write down all tasks and responsibilities you currently face.

2. Assess Urgency and Importance: Evaluate each task based on urgency and importance.

3. Categorize Tasks: Place each task into one of the four quadrants of the Eisenhower Matrix.

4. Action Plan:

- Focus on completing tasks in the "Urgent and Important" quadrant immediately.

- Schedule tasks in your calendar in the "Important but Not Urgent" quadrant.

- Delegate tasks to appropriate team members in the "Urgent but Not Important" quadrant.

- Eliminate tasks in the "Neither Urgent nor Important" quadrant.

This method enhances productivity and fosters a sense of control and clarity, empowering you to navigate the complexities of your role with confidence and precision.

Delegating Tasks Effectively

Delegation is a vital management strategy that empowers team members, enhances their skills, and frees managers to focus on high-level strategic priorities. By delegating tasks thoughtfully, you create a more capable and versatile workforce while driving organizational goals forward.

To determine which tasks to delegate, assess their complexity, required skills, and alignment with your team members' strengths and development goals. Routine or administrative tasks are ideal for delegation, as they ensure operational efficiency without needing your direct involvement. Additionally, delegating tasks that match your team members' aspirations provides valuable opportunities for growth and career advancement.

When determining which tasks to delegate to whom, it is imperative to match the task requirements with your team members' capabilities and developmental objectives. This alignment ensures the task is executed proficiently and contributes to the individual's professional development. For instance, delegating a complex data-driven project to them would be mutually beneficial if you have a team member who excels in data analysis and is keen on advancing their analytical skills. Additionally, consider the impact of delegation on the team's workload and dynamics, ensuring that the distribution of tasks does not overwhelm any individual and maintains a harmonious workflow. The last thing you want to do is reduce your feeling of being overwhelmed at the expense of one of your team members.

Effective delegation is a structured process that begins with clearly defining the task and its expected outcomes. This involves providing detailed instructions, specifying the objectives, and outlining the desired results. Clarity in communication is paramount to ensure that the team member fully understands the task and the standards by which it should be completed. Following this, it is crucial to provide the necessary resources and support to facilitate the successful completion of the task. This may include access to relevant tools, training, or information the team member may require. Setting realistic deadlines and establishing checkpoints for progress review are essential components of effective delegation. Regular check-ins allow you to monitor progress, address challenges, and provide constructive feedback, ensuring that the task stays on track and meets the desired standards.

I remember overseeing a major project launch, and I knew I couldn't handle every detail alone. To best use our team's diverse skills, I carefully broke down the project into core components: market research, content creation, and campaign management. I decided to delegate these areas based on each team member's strengths and interests.

For instance, I assigned the market research aspect to Alex, who had a knack for data analysis and was eager to deepen his skills in that area. Content creation went to Sarah, our go-to for anything creative, as she had a talent for crafting engaging narratives that aligned perfectly with our brand's tone. By matching tasks with their skills and career goals, I knew they'd handle their roles proficiently and find the work fulfilling.

I gave each person clear instructions and the resources needed to succeed. We set up regular check-ins, which allowed me to monitor progress, address any obstacles, and offer guidance where required. This approach helped lighten my workload, but more importantly, it allowed Alex and Sarah to step up, own their responsibilities, and develop their skills further. Ultimately, the project launch was successful, and the team felt more cohesive and motivated. This experience showed me the value of thoughtful delegation—getting things done and empowering my team.

Role-playing exercises can further refine your delegation skills. Envision a scenario where you must delegate a complex task, such as developing a new client proposal. Begin by clearly outlining the task, including the objectives, expected outcomes, and any specific requirements. Identify a team member whose skills and career goals align with the task and provide them with the necessary resources and support. Establish a timeline with regular checkpoints to review progress and offer feedback. Engage in a role-playing exercise with a colleague or mentor, practicing the delegation process and refining your approach based on their feedback. Reflect on past delegation experiences, considering what worked well and could be improved. This reflective practice will enhance your ability to delegate effectively, ensuring that tasks are distributed to maximize efficiency and foster team development.

Reflective prompts can also aid in honing your delegation skills. Consider a recent instance where you delegated a task. Reflect on the clarity of your instructions, your support, and the outcomes achieved. Identify any challenges encountered and how they were addressed. Consider how the delegation process impacted the team member's development and confidence. Use these reflections to identify areas for improvement and develop strategies for more effective delegation in the future. Continuously refining your delegation skills will create a more dynamic and capable team, enabling you to focus on strategic initiatives and drive organizational success.

Balancing Work and Personal Life

Maintaining a harmonious work-life balance is a fundamental pillar for sustained productivity and overall well-being in the intricate dance of professional and personal responsibilities. The relentless pace of contemporary work environments often propels managers into a vortex of tasks, deadlines, and obligations, leading to an insidious erosion of boundaries between professional duties and personal time. This blurring of lines can precipitate burnout, a chronic stress characterized by exhaustion, cynicism, and diminished efficacy. Proactively cultivating a balanced lifestyle can mitigate these adverse effects, fostering a healthier, more fulfilling existence. Reducing burnout and stress is paramount, as chronic stress not only undermines mental and physical health but also diminishes cognitive function, creativity, and decision-making abilities. Furthermore, a well-balanced life enhances job satisfaction, as individuals who allocate time for personal pursuits, leisure activities, and self-care are more likely to experience a sense of fulfillment and contentment. This equilibrium also enriches personal and professional relationships, enabling you to engage more meaningfully with family, friends, and colleagues, strengthening the social fabric that underpins emotional resilience and support.

To achieve this elusive balance, it is imperative to implement specific strategies that delineate the boundaries between work and personal time. Setting clear boundaries for work hours is a crucial first step. Establishing a defined start and end to your workday and adhering to these limits ensures that work does not infringe on personal time. This may involve setting up automated email responses outside work hours or communicating your availability to colleagues and supervisors. Prioritizing self-care and leisure activities is equally important. Engaging in regular exercise, pursuing hobbies, and spending quality time with loved ones are not mere indulgences but essential components of a balanced life. These activities provide respite from work-related stress, rejuvenating the mind and body. Scheduling regular downtime and vacations is another vital strategy. By planning and taking periodic breaks, you allow yourself the opportunity to recharge and return to work with renewed vigor and perspective.

Nevertheless, maintaining a work-life balance is not without its challenges. One of the most common obstacles is managing expectations from superiors and team members. The pressure to meet targets, deliver results, and be constantly available can create a pervasive sense of obligation that infringes on personal time. To navigate this, it is essential to communicate effectively and assertively, setting realistic expectations and boundaries with your superiors and team. Handling work-related stress and pressure is another significant challenge. Stress management techniques, such as mindfulness, deep breathing exercises, and time management strategies, can help alleviate work-related stress. Balancing remote work and home responsibilities, particularly in the current climate of increased remote work, presents an additional layer of complexity. Creating a dedicated workspace, establishing a routine, and setting clear boundaries between work and home life are critical in managing this balance.

Reflective exercises can be valuable tools for assessing and improving your work-life balance. Take a moment to reflect on your current work-life balance, considering areas where you feel overwhelmed or where personal time is compromised. Identify specific actions you can take to address these imbalances, such as setting more precise boundaries, delegating tasks, or scheduling regular downtime.

To create a balanced weekly schedule, start by outlining your work commitments and identifying periods of high demand. Allocate specific times for personal activities, ensuring that you have regular intervals for self-care and leisure. Incorporate flexibility into your schedule to accommodate unforeseen demands, but remain steadfast in protecting your personal time. By conscientiously planning and adhering to a balanced schedule, you can navigate work and personal life demands with greater ease and resilience.

Balancing work and personal life is an ongoing effort that requires setting boundaries, prioritizing self-care, and addressing challenges as they arise. Achieving this balance enhances productivity, well-being, and overall quality of life. In the next chapter, we'll explore strategies for managing remote teams effectively, focusing on maintaining productivity and cohesion in virtual environments.

Downloadable Resources

To complement this chapter, the following resources are available for download at the end of Chapter 15:

a. The Eisenhower Matrix– A worksheet to help you assess and improve organizing priorities.

b. Link to Break Free scorecard

c. Use wheel of life

d. Daily Planner

e. Weekly planner

f. Weekly task planner

Make a Difference with Your Review

"Leadership is not about being in charge. It's about taking care of those in your charge." – Simon Sinek

Are you ready to help someone take charge of their leadership journey?

By sharing your thoughts on Master Management and leadership Skills, you could help someone transform their leadership approach and achieve their goals.

Most people decide whether to read a book based on reviews. By leaving your review, you could make a profound difference. Your words could help:

- One more leader communicate more effectively with their team.

- One more manager achieve balance in their professional and personal life.

- One more professional overcome stress and lead with confidence.

- One more person inspire their team to reach new heights.

Reviewing is quick, free, and takes less than 60 seconds. Yet, the impact of your words could ripple through workplaces and teams worldwide. **If you'd like to make a difference, here's how:**

- Click on the link here Or scan the QR code

Wendy

P.S. – Your review could be the spark that ignites someone's leadership journey. Thank you for taking a moment to help others grow!

Managing Remote Teams

In the early days of her tenure as the head of a globally dispersed software development team, Vanessa faced an unexpected challenge: the rapid shift to remote work brought on by COVID-19. Staring at a screen filled with avatars, each representing a team member scattered across different time zones, she realized her role was not just about managing projects but about building a cohesive unit that could collaborate effectively despite the physical distance. The pandemic amplified the complexities of ensuring seamless communication and collaboration, making it clear that her team's success would depend on the tools and strategies she chose to deploy. This chapter explores the intricacies of managing remote teams, starting with the essential tools that make virtual collaboration possible.

Tools for Remote Communication and Collaboration

The thoughtful selection and use of advanced communication and collaboration tools greatly enhance the success of remote teams. Video conferencing platforms such as Zoom and Microsoft Teams have become essential, offering features like high-quality video calls, screen-sharing, and virtual meeting rooms that mimic the experience of in-person interactions. These platforms enable regular team meetings, one-on-one check-ins, and larger gatherings like webinars and training sessions. Zoom, for example, supports up to 100 participants on its free plan, with a 40-minute meeting limit. In contrast, paid plans offer additional features such as call recording and breakout rooms for smaller group discussions.

Team Meetings

Instant messaging tools like Slack and Glip offer robust solutions for asynchronous communication, enabling team members to exchange messages, share files, and collaborate on projects in real-time. Slack's customizable notifications, video chats, and audio calls make it a versatile platform for constant communication without requiring lengthy email threads. Its integration capabilities with various other apps enhance productivity by centralizing work processes. Glip, on the other hand, stands out for its seamless video chat experience and task management features, offering a cleaner interface that supports calendar synchronization and file access.

Project management software like Asana and Trello is pivotal in organizing tasks, setting deadlines, and tracking progress. With its detailed project planning and timeline features, Asana allows managers to assign tasks, monitor completion rates, and ensure that projects stay on track. Trello's visual interface, characterized by boards and columns, provides a user-friendly way to manage tasks, delegate responsibilities, and collaborate on projects. Both platforms offer free versions with essential features, while their paid plans unlock advanced functionalities such as automation, integrations, and enhanced security.

Selecting the right tools for your team requires a clear understanding of their needs and preferences. Ease of use and an intuitive user interface is essential to ensure that all team members can navigate the tools effortlessly, regardless of their technical proficiency. Integration with existing systems is another key consideration, as tools that seamlessly fit into your current workflow can significantly enhance productivity and reduce the learning curve. Security and privacy features are also critical, particularly given the prevalence of cyber threats. Choosing tools that comply with industry standards and offer robust encryption and access controls is vital for protecting sensitive information.

Maximizing the effectiveness of remote tools involves establishing clear communication protocols, scheduling regular check-ins, and setting up dedicated channels for different topics and projects. Clear communication protocols outline the preferred communication channels, such as instant messaging for quick updates and video conferencing for detailed discussions. Regular check-ins and virtual meetings help maintain a sense of connection and ensure everyone is aligned with the team's goals. Setting up channels or groups for different projects within tools like Slack or Microsoft Teams organizes communication, making tracking discussions and retrieving information easier.

Ensuring all team members can effectively use the selected tools is essential for optimal collaboration. Comprehensive training sessions at the outset can help familiarize everyone with the tools' functionalities and best practices. Providing user guides and FAQs offers a valuable resource for team members to consult when they encounter issues or need clarification. Offering ongoing support and troubleshooting, whether through dedicated IT support or peer assistance programs, ensures that technical challenges are promptly resolved, minimizing disruptions to the workflow.

Resource List: Essential Tools for Remote Teams

- Video Conferencing Platforms: Zoom, Microsoft Teams, Skype

- Instant Messaging Tools: Slack, Glip, Microsoft Teams

- Project Management Software: Asana, Trello, Basecamp

These tools and strategies will enable you to build a cohesive, productive, and secure remote team capable of achieving remarkable results without physical proximity.

Virtual team-building activities are one of the most effective ways to foster team cohesion remotely. These activities are not merely recreational; they serve the critical function of bringing team members together and nurturing a sense of camaraderie. Online games and quizzes, for instance, can provide a fun and engaging way for team members to interact and bond. Platforms like Kahoot! and Quizizz offer a plethora of customizable quizzes that can be tailored to your team's interests and preferences, making them both enjoyable and relevant. Virtual coffee breaks and social hours are another excellent way to foster informal interactions, allowing team members to connect personally and discuss topics beyond work-related matters. These sessions can be scheduled regularly, providing a consistent opportunity for team bonding. Collaborative projects and workshops, on the other hand, offer a more structured approach to team-building, encouraging team members to work together towards a common goal and fostering a sense of collective achievement.

Regular communication and engagement are the foundation of any remote team. Consistent and meaningful interaction keeps the team connected and aligned with the organization's goals. Practices like daily stand-ups and weekly check-ins help ensure everyone is on the same page, aware of progress and informed about any challenges. Conducting these meetings via video calls can add a personal touch, allowing team members to see each other's expressions and body language. This visual connection significantly enhances understanding and empathy while allowing one to address concerns or issues in real-time, fostering responsiveness and collaboration.

Building a positive remote culture requires intentional and ongoing effort. Celebrating team achievements and milestones is a powerful way to acknowledge and reinforce positive behaviors and outcomes. Recognizing successes, whether completing a project or reaching a key milestone, boosts morale and motivation. Promoting diversity and inclusion initiatives is equally important, as it ensures all team members feel valued and respected, enhancing their engagement and commitment. Sharing personal updates and stories contributes to a positive remote culture by humanizing team members and fostering a sense of connection. Updates about individual achievements, hobbies, or even challenges help build stronger relationships and deepen empathy among team members.

Virtual Team-Building Activity Checklist

- Online Games and Quizzes: Use platforms like Kahoot! and Quizizz to engage the team.

- Virtual Coffee Breaks: Schedule regular informal sessions for personal interaction.

- Collaborative Projects: Organize workshops and projects that require teamwork and collective effort.

- Celebrating Achievements: Acknowledge and celebrate team milestones and successes.

- Diversity and Inclusion: Promote initiatives that foster a diverse and inclusive environment.

- Personal Updates: Encourage sharing of personal stories and achievements to build connections.

Integrating these strategies and activities into your remote team management practices can maintain team cohesion and create a supportive and engaging remote work environment.

Ensuring Productivity in Remote Teams

Setting clear expectations and goals remotely is paramount to maintaining productivity and alignment. Establishing key performance indicators (KPIs) provides a concrete framework for assessing progress and identifying improvement areas. These metrics should be specific, measurable, and aligned with organizational objectives. For instance, a sales manager might set KPIs around monthly revenue targets, customer acquisition rates, and client retention metrics. Detailed project plans and timelines further delineate responsibilities and deadlines, ensuring that each team member understands their role and the broader timeline of deliverables. This structure clarifies expectations and mitigates the ambiguity plaguing remote work environments.

Monitoring performance and providing feedback are critical components of effective remote team management. Performance tracking tools, such as time management software and project tracking platforms, offer real-time insights into individual and team progress. Regular performance reviews serve as formal checkpoints to discuss achievements, challenges, and areas for growth. However, the spontaneity of real-time feedback cannot be overlooked; providing immediate support and guidance can address issues before they escalate, fostering a culture of continuous improvement. For example, a project manager might use software like Monday.com to track task completion and provide instant feedback, ensuring that project milestones are met consistently.

Encouraging self-discipline and accountability within remote teams necessitates a multifaceted approach. Time management techniques, such as the Pomodoro Technique and time-blocking, can help team members structure their workdays effectively. Encouraging productivity tools, like digital task lists and calendars, instill a sense of responsibility and organization. Task management apps like Todoist or calendar integrations in tools like Google Workspace can help team members prioritize and manage their tasks efficiently. Managers can cultivate a team with autonomy and accountability by fostering an environment where self-motivation is rewarded.

Balancing flexibility with productivity is a delicate yet crucial endeavor. Flexible work hours allow team members to work during peak productivity, accommodating different time zones and personal commitments. Allowing autonomy in task management empowers team members to approach their work in the manner they find most compelling, fostering creativity and ownership. However, setting clear boundaries to separate work and personal life is equally important, preventing burnout and ensuring sustained productivity. For instance, encouraging team members to establish a dedicated workspace and adhere to regular work hours can significantly enhance focus and efficiency.

Performance Tracking Tool Comparison

- Monday.com: Real-time task tracking, customizable dashboards, integration with other tools.

- Asana: Detailed project planning, timeline features, and task assignment.

- Trello: Visual interface, boards and columns, easy task delegation.

Managers can create an environment where remote teams thrive by setting clear expectations, monitoring performance, encouraging self-discipline, and balancing flexibility with productivity. This comprehensive approach enhances individual accountability and fosters a cohesive and productive remote workforce.

Overcoming Challenges of Remote Management

Remote teams often face unique challenges that can disrupt smooth operations. Communication barriers and misunderstandings are common due to the lack of face-to-face interactions, leading to misinterpretations and a loss of contextual understanding. The nuances of body language, tone, and immediate feedback are often absent in text-based communication, amplifying these issues. Instant messaging platforms are ideal for quick updates and informal interactions, while emails are better suited for more detailed and formal communication. Maintaining team morale and engagement in a remote setting is another significant challenge. Without the physical camaraderie of an in-person workplace, team members may experience feelings of isolation, diminished motivation, and a reduced sense of belonging. Overcoming these challenges requires a thoughtful combination of technological tools and human-focused strategies. Building a solid sense of cohesion is essential for fostering effective teamwork, innovation, and productivity.

Implementing regular feedback loops ensures continuous and bidirectional communication. By scheduling periodic check-ins and feedback sessions, managers can address concerns, provide guidance, and reinforce positive behaviors in real-time. Communication skills training can further empower team members to express themselves clearly and listen actively, reducing the likelihood of misunderstandings and fostering a more collaborative environment.

Technical issues, while often unavoidable, can be minimized with robust support systems. Providing access to reliable IT support is essential, ensuring that team members have a dependable resource to turn to when encountering technical difficulties. Remote troubleshooting guides and resources can empower team members to resolve common issues on their own, reducing downtime and disruptions. Reliable internet connectivity and equipment are equally critical. Managers can help by offering stipends for high-speed internet plans or providing necessary hardware, such as routers and laptops, to ensure team members have the tools they need to work efficiently.

Maintaining team morale and motivation in a remote environment requires intentional and sustained effort. Recognizing and rewarding achievements, whether through formal recognition programs or spontaneous acknowledgments, can significantly boost morale. Celebrating milestones, big and small, fosters a sense of accomplishment and motivates team members to aim for excellence. Offering opportunities for professional development is another powerful motivator. Providing access to online courses, workshops, and training programs supports team members' growth and career advancement, increasing their engagement and commitment. Creating a supportive and inclusive work environment is equally important. Encouraging open communication, promoting diversity and inclusion, and fostering a culture of empathy and respect help create a positive atmosphere where team members feel valued and heard.

In conclusion, overcoming remote management challenges requires a comprehensive approach that addresses communication barriers, technical issues, and team morale. By leveraging multiple communication channels, providing robust technical support, and fostering a positive and inclusive work environment, managers can create a thriving remote team that is both productive and engaged. As we transition to the next chapter, we will explore the principles of continuous learning and professional development, examining how managers can foster a culture of growth and innovation within their teams.

Continuous Learning and Professional Development

In a bustling café, amidst the aroma of freshly brewed coffee, a group of managers gathered for an informal discussion. Among them was Alex, a diligent supervisor who had recently transitioned into a managerial role. As the conversation meandered through various topics, it gravitated toward personal development plans (PDPs). Intrigued, Alex listened intently, realizing that while he had excelled in his previous role, becoming an exceptional manager required a structured approach to continuous learning and professional growth. This chapter delves into the intricacies of creating and harnessing a Personal Development Plan to elevate your career trajectory.

Learn and Grow

Creating a Personal Development Plan

The significance of a Personal Development Plan cannot be overstated. It serves as a strategic blueprint, meticulously charting your path towards professional excellence. A PDP is not merely a document; it is a dynamic tool that provides clear direction and focus, helping you navigate the complexities of your career with precision. By delineating your objectives and breaking them down into actionable steps, a PDP aids in identifying both your strengths and areas necessitating improvement, fostering a culture of self-awareness and continuous growth.

The first step in crafting an effective PDP is setting SMART goals—Specific, Measurable, Achievable, Relevant, and Time-bound goals tailored to your career aspirations. This process begins with a thorough self-assessment to identify skill gaps. For a detailed guide on self-assessment tools like SWOT analysis, refer back to Chapter 1.

Next, identify resources and opportunities to support your growth. These might include advanced training programs, workshops, certifications, and mentorship opportunities. Leveraging these resources allows you to address gaps identified during your self-assessment, strengthening your skill set and enhancing your professional competence.

Regularly reviewing and updating your Personal Development Plan (PDP) is essential. A dynamic PDP ensures it stays aligned with your evolving career goals and the shifting demands of your professional environment. Conducting quarterly reviews can help you assess your progress and recalibrate your goals, keeping you on track and driving continuous improvement.

Feedback sessions with peers, mentors, and supervisors also provide valuable insights to refine your goals and strategies. Constructive feedback highlights blind spots and areas for improvement you might have overlooked. Engaging in open and honest dialogues during these sessions fosters clarity and reinforces a growth-oriented mindset. Use this feedback to adjust your PDP, ensuring it remains relevant and supports your career trajectory.

I've always believed in the importance of continuous learning and personal development. In one career phase, I set quarterly goals to strengthen my leadership abilities, just as I might advise others. My development plan (PDP) included completing a leadership certification course, attending industry events, and actively seeking mentorship opportunities. By regularly assessing my progress and seeking feedback, I identified areas for growth and refined my approach. The result was increased confidence, skill, and recognition from my peers and superiors, which opened doors to new responsibilities.

Even now, I continue to learn and develop—I'm currently enrolled in a training course and working with a coach. No matter your age, you're never too old to learn and improve.

> "Live as if you were to die tomorrow. Learn as if you were to live forever."
> – Mahatma Gandhi

To ensure the efficacy of your PDP, it is essential to remain committed and proactive. Regularly engage in self-reflection to assess your progress and make necessary adjustments. Embrace a growth mindset, viewing challenges as opportunities for learning and development. You can continuously refine your skills and achieve your professional aspirations by actively seeking feedback and leveraging available resources.

Reflection Exercise: Crafting Your Personal Development Plan

1. Set SMART Goals: Identify what you want to achieve in the short, mid, and long term.

2. Conduct a Self-Assessment: Utilize tools like SWOT analysis to identify your strengths, weaknesses, opportunities, and threats.

3. Identify Resources: List training programs, workshops, certifications, and mentorship opportunities

4. Review and Update: Schedule quarterly reviews to assess progress and recalibrate your goals.

5. Incorporate Feedback: Regularly seek feedback from peers, mentors, and supervisors to refine your PDP.

The journey toward continuous learning and professional development is an ongoing process that demands dedication, self-awareness, and strategic planning. By creating and diligently following a Personal Development Plan, you can confidently navigate the complexities of your career, ensuring sustained growth and success.

Leveraging Online Courses and ResourcesIn the quiet corner of his home office, Daniel, a dedicated project manager, often juggled multiple responsibilities, from overseeing team deliverables to attending high-stakes meetings. Amidst this whirlwind, the prospect of professional development seemed daunting until he discovered the transformative potential of online learning. The flexibility and convenience of online courses allowed Daniel to learn at his own pace, integrating new skills seamlessly into his demanding schedule. This modality offers unparalleled access to various topics and expertise, empowering professionals to expand their knowledge base without the constraints of traditional classroom settings.

Choosing the right online learning platforms is essential to ensure your time and effort result in meaningful development. Platforms like Coursera provide access to courses from prestigious universities, offering certificates and even degree programs. Udemy is an excellent choice for one-off classes on various topics, making it ideal for targeted skill acquisition. LinkedIn Learning, available with a LinkedIn membership, focuses on business skills and software training, while edX offers courses from top universities, many of which are free. To select the best courses, consider their ratings and reviews, as these often reflect the quality and relevance of the content. Additionally, pay attention to the instructor's credentials and experience, as these can significantly impact the learning experience.

Maximizing your engagement with online courses requires a proactive approach. Setting a regular study schedule is fundamental. Allocate specific times during the week dedicated solely to learning, whether early mornings, lunch breaks, or evenings. Consistency ensures steady progress and helps you assimilate new information effectively. Actively participating in discussions and assignments is equally important. Engaging with fellow learners through forums and group projects enhances comprehension and fosters a sense of community and collaboration. This interaction can provide diverse perspectives and insights, enriching your learning experience.

Integrating online learning into your daily routine may seem challenging, but with strategic planning, it becomes manageable. Allocate specific times for learning, such as early mornings or lunch breaks, to ensure that it becomes a habitual part of your day. Using mobile apps for learning on-the-go can also be advantageous. Platforms like Coursera, LinkedIn Learning, and Udemy offer mobile applications that enable you to access course materials and participate in discussions from anywhere. This flexibility allows you to utilize otherwise idle moments, such as during commutes or waiting periods.

Resource List: Top Online Learning Platforms

- Coursera: Access to university courses and degrees and free and paid options is available.

- Udemy: Wide range of one-off courses, pricing per class.

- LinkedIn Learning: Business skills and software training are included with a LinkedIn membership.

- edX: Courses from top universities are often free of charge.

Leveraging these platforms allows you to tailor your learning journey to your needs and career goals. The flexibility and convenience of online learning, combined with a proactive approach to engagement and integration into daily routines, can significantly enhance your professional development, equipping you with the skills and knowledge necessary to excel in your field.

Staying Updated with Industry Trends

Staying current with industry trends is not just beneficial; it is imperative. The business landscape continually evolves, influenced by technological advancements, market shifts, and emerging consumer behaviors. For managers, keeping abreast of these changes enhances decision-making and strategic planning. It ensures that your skills and knowledge remain relevant and competitive, allowing you to anticipate and adapt to new challenges and opportunities effectively. Without this vigilance, one risks becoming obsolete, unable to navigate the complexities of modern business environments.

Various sources can be invaluable for staying informed about the latest trends. Industry-specific journals and magazines provide deep insights and analyses from experts, offering a wealth of information on new developments and best practices. Professional associations and organizations often publish reports, hold conferences, and offer seminars that delve into the nuances of industry trends, providing both knowledge and networking opportunities. Online forums and communities are also essential, as they foster discussions and exchanges of ideas among professionals across the globe, often highlighting practical, real-world applications of theoretical concepts. Engaging with these sources regularly can keep you at the forefront of your field, equipped with the latest knowledge to drive innovation and strategic growth.

Making the practice of staying updated a regular habit requires a structured approach. Subscribing to industry newsletters and blogs is a simple yet effective way to receive updates directly in your inbox, ensuring you never miss critical information. Setting aside dedicated time for reading and research, perhaps as part of your daily or weekly routine, can help you stay consistently informed. This could be as simple as allocating 30 minutes each morning to read the latest articles or spending an hour each week delving into comprehensive reports and studies. Creating a habit of continuous learning broadens your understanding and enhances your ability to make informed decisions swiftly and confidently.

Consider the example of a marketing manager who actively engages with industry journals, professional communities, and emerging technologies. This manager can implement innovative strategies that dramatically optimize campaign performance and audience targeting by staying informed about advancements in artificial intelligence, data analytics, and automation. AI, in particular, has become a powerful tool across all management areas, transforming how we work by enabling the automation of complex processes, providing deeper insights, and facilitating data-driven decisions with unprecedented precision. Managers who embrace AI and other emerging technologies are better positioned to drive innovation, enhance team productivity, and meet evolving consumer and business needs. These scenarios illustrate the tangible benefits of staying current with industry trends. In a world where technology continuously reshapes the landscape, those who adapt and adopt transformative tools like AI will lead their teams and organizations toward lasting success and growth.

One book I've always ensured my team reads, no matter where I've worked, is *"Who Moved My Cheese?"* by Dr. Spencer Johnson. This simple yet profound story about two mice and two tiny humans navigating change in a maze holds timeless lessons about adaptability, resilience, and embracing the unknown. The characters' responses to sudden change are powerful metaphors for how we handle shifts in our personal and professional lives. In a world where change is constant, this book teaches the importance of agility and maintaining a growth mindset, highlighting that those who learn to adapt and seek new opportunities are the ones who thrive. It's a pivotal read for anyone committed to personal development, as it reinforces the value of staying open to new paths and finding the courage to let go of outdated habits or mindsets.

Engaging with industry trends also involves practical application. For instance, a manager who follows trends in remote work technology might implement new collaboration tools that enhance team productivity and communication. Adopting these technologies early can create a more efficient and cohesive remote working environment, giving the team a competitive edge.

Ultimately, staying updated with industry trends is a multifaceted endeavor that requires consistent effort and a proactive mindset. By leveraging various sources of information, making the practice of staying informed a regular habit, and applying new knowledge to real-world scenarios, you can ensure that you remain at the cutting edge of your field, well-equipped to navigate the complexities of modern business environments and lead your team to sustained success.

Participating in Professional Networks and Communities

Until recently, I hosted a local networking group that grew significantly over 12 months. Each meeting brought together professionals from diverse backgrounds, offering valuable networking and insights from guest speakers who were experts in their fields. We shared market updates, trends, and practical advice from those with real-world experience. The discussions were rich with knowledge, new perspectives, and invaluable connections. This experience underscored the power of professional networks in expanding skills, discovering new tools, and uncovering career opportunities that might otherwise stay hidden.

Identifying relevant networks and communities is the first step toward harnessing these benefits. Industry-specific associations and LinkedIn groups are excellent starting points. These platforms often host a wealth of information and activities tailored to your field, from webinars and workshops to discussion forums and job postings. Additionally, joining local and international professional organizations can broaden your horizons, offering opportunities to connect with industry leaders and experts from various geographies. These organizations frequently organize events, publish insightful articles, and provide certification programs that can enhance your professional credibility.

Active participation in these networks is crucial to reap their full benefits. Attending conferences, seminars, and webinars allows you to stay updated on the latest trends and developments while providing a platform to showcase your expertise (Robinson, 2022).[1] Contributing to discussions and sharing insights establishes you as a thought leader and fosters a collaborative environment where knowledge is freely exchanged. Volunteering for leadership roles within the community can further enhance your visibility and influence, opening avenues for career advancement and professional growth. By taking on responsibilities such as organizing events, leading committees, or mentoring new members, you demonstrate your commitment to the community and expand your network of influential contacts.

To maximize the benefits of networking, it is essential to approach it with a strategic mindset. Identify the key individuals and organizations that can add value to your professional journey and make a concerted effort to engage with them. Remember that networking is a two-way street; while seeking knowledge and opportunities, be prepared to offer your insights and assistance to others. This reciprocal approach fosters strong, mutually beneficial relationships that can endure throughout your career.

In conclusion, participating in professional networks and communities is a powerful strategy for continuous learning and professional development. Expanding your knowledge through peer learning, gaining access to new opportunities and resources, and actively engaging with relevant networks can significantly enhance your professional growth and career trajectory.

Practical Tools and Exercises for Managers

As you've journeyed through the strategies and skills discussed in this book, you now have a toolkit of practical management resources. This chapter is designed as a quick reference, highlighting the tools, exercises, and frameworks explored throughout the book. For each tool, you'll find a reminder of its purpose and a link to the chapter where it's discussed in detail. Downloadable resources are provided at the end of this chapter to give you practical, hands-on support.

Chapter 1. Foundations of Effective Management

SWOT Analysis and SMART Goals Framework

- Use the SWOT Analysis to identify strengths, weaknesses, opportunities, and threats.

https://bit.ly/SWOTanalysisRSP

- SMART goals to structure and prioritize your development effectively.

https://bit.ly/SMARTRSP

Chapter 3. Emotional Intelligence in Management

Emotional Intelligence (EQ) Development Tools

- Emotional Intelligence Self-Assessment and EQ Exercises: Strengthen self-awareness, empathy, and interpersonal skills to become an emotionally intelligent manager.

https://blossomup.co/

- Manager's Journal, explicitly designed for this book, is available on Amazon.

https://mybook.to/Journal-manager-growth

Chapter 6. Decision-Making Skills

Decision-Making Rational

- Structured Decision-Making Framework. A clear framework to improve decision-making by evaluating options and outcomes logically.

https://bit.ly/Decision-making-rational

Chapter 7. Building High-Performing Teams

PDCA Worksheet (Plan, Do, Check, Act)

- PDCA Cycle Worksheet: A continuous improvement process to enhance productivity and performance through iterative planning and review.

https://bit.ly/RPCAcycle

Chapter 9. Transitioning from Manager to Leader

100% Standard & DISC Assessment

- What Does 100% Look Like? Define clear standards for performance.

https://bit.ly/whatdoes100looklikeRSP

- DISC Personality Assessment: For better understanding and collaboration.

https://www.tonyrobbins.com/disc

Chapter 12. *Effective Time Management*

Time Management & Productivity Tools

- Eisenhower Matrix: Optimize time management through prioritization.

https://bit.ly/theeisenhowermatrix

- Wheel of Life: Better understand and balance life areas.

https://bit.ly/wheeloflifeRSP

- Breakfree ScoreApp: Discover how procrastination affects your life.

https://procrastination.scoreapp.com/

Additional Resources:

- Daily Planner

https://bit.ly/DailyplannerRSP

- Weekly Planner

https://bit.ly/WeeklyplannerRSP

- Task Planner: to organize and structure tasks effectively.

https://bit.ly/weeklytaskplannerRSP

Chapter 14. Continuous Learning and Professional Development

Personal Development Plan (PDP)

- PDP Goal Setting and Action Plan: Establish a structured personal development plan with actionable growth and career progression steps.

https://bit.ly/personaldevelopmentplanRSP

Accessing Your Downloadable Resources

All the downloadable resources mentioned in this chapter, including templates, worksheets, and planners, are available via the links and QR codes below. These resources will help you implement the strategies and frameworks discussed in the book as practical guides in your day-to-day management practices. Scan the QR code or click on the link to access each tool:

Final Note

This toolkit is intended to smooth your management journey by providing easy access to the resources you need. Revisit this chapter as needed, and remember that effective management is an evolving skill set. Use these tools to reinforce the strategies in this book, fostering a habit of continuous improvement and growth in your role.

Conclusion

As we come to the end of this journey. I want to take a moment to reflect on the key themes that have guided us. From our first discussions on the foundations of effective management to exploring the complexities of ethical leadership, communication, team building, and decision-making, each chapter has aimed to unpack what it truly means to be a successful manager. These insights aren't just theories but practical lessons I've gathered and applied throughout my career. I hope these pages have given you the tools and confidence to navigate your own unique path as a manager.

We commenced our journey with a detailed examination of the **Foundations of Effective Management,** where we underscored the critical importance of understanding your role as a manager, identifying your management style, and employing self-evaluation tools. The pivotal concepts of setting clear expectations and goals, building trust and credibility, and mastering time management techniques were elucidated, forming the bedrock upon which all subsequent skills are built.

Our inquiry then ventured into **Communication Skills**, emphasizing the quintessential practices of active listening, crafting clear and concise messages, providing constructive feedback, and navigating difficult conversations. These skills are paramount for transmitting information and fostering an environment of openness, trust, and mutual respect.

In the **Emotional Intelligence in Management chapter,** we delved into the profound impact of self-awareness, emotional regulation, empathy, and conflict resolution. These competencies enable you to navigate your team's emotional landscapes, ensuring that interpersonal dynamics are managed with sensitivity and astuteness.

The discourse on **Ethical Leadership** illuminated the principles of integrity, transparency, and accountability. We examined ethical decision-making frameworks and the creation of an ethical workplace culture, underscoring the profound impact of ethical behavior on organizational trust and success.

The chapters on Team Building, Stress Management, and Preventing Burnout provided actionable strategies for fostering high-performing teams and maintaining well-being in high-pressure environments. We explored trust-building exercises, effective collaboration techniques, conflict-resolution strategies, and resilience-building practices, all of which aimed at creating a supportive and productive work environment.

The exploration of **Transitioning from Manager to Leader** and **Navigating Organizational Politics** offered insights into the shift from task management to inspirational leadership and the complexities of organizational power dynamics. We discussed techniques for building alliances, advocating for your team, and influencing senior leaders, equipping you with the tools to thrive in politically charged environments.

Our discussion on **Effective Time Management** and **Managing Remote Teams** provided practical frameworks and tools to enhance productivity and cohesion in physical or virtual workspaces. Techniques such as the Eisenhower Matrix, delegation skills, and remote collaboration tools were meticulously examined to ensure efficient task and team management.

Lastly, the chapters on **Continuous Learning, Professional Development,** and **Practical Tools and Exercises for Managers** emphasize the importance of lifelong learning and provide tangible resources, self-assessments, and team-building activities to foster continuous growth and improvement.

Key takeaways from this comprehensive guide are manifold and multifaceted. At the core, remember the imperative of self-awareness and continuous self-improvement, the criticality of effective communication, and the necessity of ethical leadership. Embrace the power of emotional intelligence, the strength of cohesive teams, and the wisdom of sound decision-making frameworks. Prioritize time management and adapt to the evolving demands of remote work with agility and innovation. Above all, commit to continuous learning and professional development, for it is through persistent growth that you will remain at the forefront of management excellence.

As you stand on the cusp of your next managerial challenge, I urge you to take decisive action. Reflect on the insights from these chapters, implement the strategies discussed, and strive to embody the principles of exemplary management and leadership principles. A manager's journey is one of perpetual evolution, marked by the relentless pursuit of excellence and the unwavering commitment to the well-being and success of your team.

Let us acknowledge the transformative power of excellent management and leadership. A manager who leads with integrity, empathy, and vision drives organizational success and inspires and uplifts those around them. Your role as a manager is to oversee tasks and ignite potential, foster innovation, and cultivate a culture of trust and collaboration. As you navigate the complexities of your managerial journey, may you do so with courage, conviction, and an unyielding dedication to excellence.

Thank you for embarking on this journey with me. May the insights and strategies shared within these pages serve as a compass, guiding you toward a future of impactful and inspiring leadership.

Thank You for Reading *Master Management & Leadership Skills*

Congratulations on completing your journey through this guide to advanced management and leadership. I hope the tools and strategies you've learned will empower you to confidently lead, inspire your team, and achieve lasting success in your career.

"True leadership is not about authority but about inspiring growth and creating a shared vision for success." (Chapter 7: Trust is the foundation of effective team dynamics)

If this book has provided valuable insights, practical strategies, or a fresh perspective on management, I would be grateful if you could share your feedback on Amazon. Your review will help others discover this book and encourage them to take the next step in their leadership journey.

How to Leave a Review:

1. Visit the Amazon page where you purchased this book.

2. Share your experience—what strategies you implemented, what resonated most, and how the book impacted your leadership journey.

3. Even a short review makes a significant difference!

Thank you for taking the time to share your thoughts and helping others become confident, effective leaders. Together, we can inspire growth, one leader at a time.

Thank you for being a part of this journey. Your support is a step that impacts the lives of others.

Scan the QR code to take you to the book review page.

Citations

Foundations of Effective Management

1. Evans, R. (2022). *Understanding management styles*. Leadership Dynamics.

2. Garcia, P. (2021). *Self-evaluation for continuous improvement*. Growth Strategies.

3. Martinez, S. (2020). *SMART goals: Setting effective objectives*. Goal-Setting Publications.

Mastering Communication Skills

1. Garcia, P. (2021). *Techniques for enhancing active listening*. Listening Skills Publishers.

2. Evans, R. (2021). *Using visual aids to enhance clarity*. Visual Communication Review.

3. Harris, D. (2022). *Preparing for difficult conversations with empathy*. Emotional Intelligence Review.

Emotional Intelligence in Management

1. Martinez, S. (2022). *Mindfulness techniques for managing emotions under pressure*. Mindful Leadership House.

2. Evans, R. (2021). *The importance of support systems in emotional regulation*. Workplace Wellness Press.

3. Johnson, A. (2023). *Empathy as a cornerstone of leadership*. Empathetic Leadership Journal.

4. Roberts, K. (2020). *Techniques to enhance empathetic leadership*. Interpersonal Skills Publishers.

Ethical Leadership

1. Evans, R. (2021). *The Utilitarian approach in ethical decision-making*. Moral Leadership House.

2. Martinez, S. (2022). *Protecting individual rights in decision-making*. Rights and Ethics Publishers.

3. Harris, D. (2021). *The fairness approach in ethical leadership*. Justice and Equity Press.

4. Roberts, K. (2020). *Steps to ethical decision-making*. Decision Ethics Journal.

Mastering Difficult Conversations

1. Evans, R. (2021). *A structured approach to delivering feedback*. Feedback Strategies House.

2. Roberts, K. (2020). *Setting SMART goals for effective feedback*. Goal Achievement Press.

Decision-Making Skills

1. Garcia, P. (2021). *Effective decision-making models for managers*. Business Frameworks Publishers.

2. Taylor, M. (2021). *Challenges of rational decision-making in fast-paced environments*. Decision Review.

3. Garcia, P. (2023). *Balancing data and intuition for better decision-making*. Insightful Managers Journal.

4. Johnson, A. (2024). *Evaluating outcomes for managerial growth*. Management Development Review.

Building High-Performing Teams

1. Deming, W. E. (1986). *Out of the Crisis*. MIT Press.

Stress Management and Preventing Burnout

1. Smith, A., & Jones, B. (2020). *Workplace Stress and Its Impact on Employee Health*. Business Insights Press.

2. Johnson, C. (2019). *Balancing Work and Life: Strategies for Employee Well-being*. Organizational Studies Journal.

3. Green, L. (2021). *Flexible Work Arrangements and Job Satisfaction*. HR Management Review.

Transitioning from Manager to Leader

1. Robbins, T. (2020). DISC assessment. Retrieved from https://www.tonyrobbins.com/disc

2. Goleman, D. (1998). *What Makes a Leader?* Harvard Business Review.

3. Rothwell, W. J. (2010). *Effective Succession Planning: Ensuring Leadership Continuity and Building Talent from Within*. AMACOM.

Navigating Organizational Politics

1. Cross, R., Ernst, C., & Pasmore, B. (2013). *A Bridge Too Far? How Boundary Spanners Help and Hinder Work Performance in Cross-Functional Teams. Organization Science*, 24(4), 1181-1198.

Effective Time Management

1. Eisenhower, D. D. (1954). *Speech at the Second Assembly of the World Council of Churches*. World Council of Churches.

Continuous Learning and Professional Development

1. Robinson, P. (2022). The value of attending seminars and conferences for professional growth. Professional Networks Magazine.